NF —

Instant Pot®
Miracle Cookbook

Instant Pot®
Miracle Cookbook

Over 150 step-by-step foolproof recipes for your electric
pressure cooker, slow cooker or Instant Pot. Fully authorised.

EBURY
PRESS

10 9 8 7 6 5 4 3 2 1

Ebury Press, an imprint of Ebury Publishing,
20 Vauxhall Bridge Road,
London, SW1V 2SA

Ebury Press is part of the Penguin Random House group of companies
whose addresses can be found at global.penguinrandomhouse.com

Penguin
Random House
UK

INSTANT POT® and the Instant Pot® logo are registered trademarks of
Double Insight Inc. Used under license.

First published by Ebury Press in 2017

www.penguin.co.uk

A CIP catalogue record for this book is available from the British Library

"Pumpkin-Spice Steel-Cut Oats," "Chickpea Broccoli Salad," "Maple &
Vinegar-Braised Parsnips," and "Spicy Brown Rice and Bean Soup" from
VEGAN UNDER PRESSURE: Perfect Vegan Meals Made Quick and Easy in
Your Pressure Cooker by Jill Nussinow, MS, RDN. Copyright © 2016 by
Jill Nussinow, MS, RDN. Used by permission of Houghton Mifflin Harcourt.
All rights reserved.

ISBN 9781785038211

Printed and bound in China by Toppan Leefung

Penguin Random House is committed to a sustainable future for our
business, our readers and our planet. This book is made from Forest
Stewardship Council® certified paper.

Contents

The Story of the Instant Pot®

The idea for the Instant Pot® – a multipurpose cooker that relies on the latest technologies – started with a simple, basic and universal desire.

In 2008, Robert Wang and two colleagues (who along with Wang would eventually be founders of the company that produces the Instant Pot®) began brainstorming ideas for kitchen appliances that could address the very personal concerns they had about being able to fix quick, healthy, delicious meals after long days at work. All three had worked in the Canadian high-tech industry. Wang's wife worked in the high-tech field as well – and the couple had two young children. There was another motivating factor: Wang and his colleagues observed changes in the lifestyles of North Americans. Although people were busier than ever and had less time to cook, they wanted to eat more healthily.

The trio settled on rebooting the pressure cooker – traditionally a casserole pot for the hob with a locked-on lid fitted with a rubber or plastic gasket and heated up until enough pressure built up in the pot to cook foods far more quickly than regular braising and steaming methods. Although once popular, pressure cooking had fallen out of favour because of tales told of exploding pots that catapulted hot beef stew or cooked beans all over the kitchen. Safety was their first hurdle. They decided to make it their top priority, followed by innovation. Their appliance would not just be a pressure cooker but also a slow cooker, rice cooker, steamer, sauté pan and yogurt maker – all in one.

They partnered with three other investors and set up a business called Double Insight in Ottawa to manufacture their brainchild. The first Instant Pot® came on the market in 2010. The rest, as they say, is history.

Word spread – primarily through social media – about the convenience the pot provides to the home cook and the creativity it allows for meal-making even on the busiest days. Nearly everyone who acquires an Instant Pot® becomes an instant fan – and they enthusiastically spread the word to friends, family members and co-workers. Words used to describe the Instant Pot® veer towards the passionate. 'Love!' and 'life-changing' are two of the most common praises.

And then of course there are the results: Butter-knife-tender roasts in minutes, creamy risottos with no stirring, hearty bean soups and chilli with no overnight soaking and a fraction of the traditional cooking time – and the creamiest, fluffiest cheesecake you will ever taste.

The creators of the Instant Pot® do not rest on their laurels and the tremendous success of their invention. They are constantly seeking to improve it based on feedback from their customers. Each iteration released to the market – every 12 to 18 months – has enhancements to make using it easier and more satisfying.

It may sound too good to be true, but it's not. With a little bit of prep work and the push of a button, you can get wonderful, healthy meals on the table with speed and ease and (dare we say) have a lot of fun doing it!

Happy cooking!

How to Use the Instant Pot®

The User Manual that came with your Instant Pot® has detailed information on how to use the appliance. Read through it and refer to it as often as necessary. Here are the basics, plus some points that should be highlighted.

The Basics

• When you plug in your Instant Pot®, the display will read **OFF**. After you have selected the cooking function and adjusted the time, if necessary, the pot will automatically go on and start cooking 10 seconds after you push the last button.
• Press **CANCEL** if you need to start over.
• Press **CANCEL** when you are switching functions in the middle of a recipe – for instance, from **SAUTÉ** to **MANUAL** or from **SLOW COOK** to **SAUTÉ** to reduce a sauce.
• For both the **SAUTÉ** and **SLOW COOK** functions, there are three temperature settings: **LESS**, **NORMAL** and **MORE**.
Note: If you have an Ultra 10-in-1 Multi-Use Programmable Pressure Cooker, Low/Medium/High correspond to Less/Normal/More on the Duo 7-in-1 Multi-Use Programmable Pressure Cooker.
• For all cooking functions except **SLOW COOK**, **YOGURT**, and **SAUTÉ** (when you don't use the lid), the pressure-release valve should be in the closed or sealed position.

Pressure Cooking in the Instant Pot®

Pressure cooking can be done in one of two ways:
The selection of **MANUAL** (choosing high or low pressure) and the setting of the cook time using the **+** and **-** buttons is one way. The other is through the use of the pre-set buttons. Each of the pre-set buttons defaults to high pressure, with the exception of **RICE**, which defaults to low pressure. Each pre-set button also has a default (**NORMAL**) cook time, but can be adjusted to **LESS** or **MORE**. Each pre-set can also be customised to any time you like using the **+** and **-** buttons. To see the **NORMAL**, **LESS** and **MORE** cook times for each pre-set function, press the **ADJUST** button to toggle among them. (Note that these times only refer to the cook time – not the Closed Pot Time; see 'Understanding the Timings', page 13.) To clear the machine from a previously customised cook time, press the **ADJUST** button for 3 seconds, until you hear a beep.

Slow Cooking in the Instant Pot®

The **SLOW COOK** function on the Instant Pot® defaults to a 4-hour cook time. Use the **+** or **-** buttons to set the time and the **ADJUST** button to toggle among the three temperature settings – **NORMAL, LESS** and **MORE**. In this book, **SLOW COOK** is most often used on **MORE**. This temperature level is the equivalent of medium-high if there was such a setting on a stand-alone slow cooker, so the timings are somewhere between what would be low and high on a regular slow cooker.

Sautéing in the Instant Pot®

The **SAUTÉ** function on the Instant Pot® has three temperature settings – **NORMAL, LESS** and **MORE**. Although you don't need to set a cook time for the **SAUTÉ** function, it automatically shuts off after 30 minutes. In this book, **SAUTÉ** is most often used on **NORMAL** (although there are few exceptions). **MORE** can be used to very quickly sear and brown a piece of meat, and **LESS** can be used to simmer or reduce a sauce.

Other Functions

The **YOGURT** programme involves a two-stage process to make homemade yogurt – first to boil and cool down the milk, then to incubate the yogurt for a minimum of 8 hours after the live cultures are added. See page 277 for the Homemade Yogurt recipe.

Use the **DELAY START** button (or **TIMER** on older models) to delay the start of cooking. Select a cooking function, make any adjustments, then press the **DELAY START** button and adjust with the **+** and **-** buttons. Press the button once for hours and again for minutes.

Use **KEEP WARM/CANCEL** to cancel a function or turn off the Instant Pot®. The **SLOW COOK** and all pressure-cooking functions switch over to **KEEP WARM** after the cook time is complete and the pressure has been released from the pot, whether by a natural or quick release.

1. To open the lid, grasp the handle and rotate lid about 30 degrees counterclockwise in the direction of 'Open' until the ▼ mark on the lid is aligned with the ▲ mark on the cooker base. When the lid can be lifted off the pot, you will hear a chime.

2. The inner pot of the Instant Pot® is removable for easy cleaning and so that you can better read the volume-level markings on the inside. You can either add the food and liquid to the inner pot when it is outside of the Instant Pot® or when it has been placed inside the Instant Pot®. Be sure the outside is clean and free of drips before you return the inner pot to the Instant Pot® for cooking.

3. For pressure cooking, the total amount of food and liquid should never exceed the maximum level marking of the inner pot. It's recommended that you do not fill the inner pot more than ⅔ full. For foods such as rice, beans and dried vegetables, do not fill pot more than ½ full.

4. Secure the lid on the pot by the opposite method of opening it. You will hear a chime when it is locked on.

Turn the pressure-release valve to the proper setting – open or closed – for your recipe.

5. Select cooking function and programme the cooker. Adjust pressure, temperature and cook times according to the directions in your recipe if necessary.

6. For pressure cooking, release the pressure in one of two ways according to what is specified in the recipe.

Quick Release: Turn the pressure-release valve to the open or venting position to quickly release steam until the float valve drops down. In general, do not use quick release for foods with a large volume of liquid or high starch content, such as grains and starchy soups. Food may splatter out of the valve.

Natural Release: Leave the pressure-release valve in the closed position. This method allows the cooker to cool down naturally until the float valve drops down. This can take 10 to 15 minutes or even longer. The cooker will not go into the **KEEP WARM** cycle until all of the pressure has been released.

How to Use Our Recipes

In addition to knowing how to use the Instant Pot® from a technical standpoint, understanding how the recipes in this book are written will make cooking with it that much easier.

Recipe Selection

With the exception of the blogger favourites, every recipe in this book was created new for the Instant Pot®. We wanted this book to be comprehensive – to be largely built on classic dishes everyone loves to make and eat adapted for the Instant Pot®. You know you can turn to this book for superlative versions of your favourite foods. But we also included a selection of innovative dishes or standards with a twist to keep things fresh and interesting. The recipes are written so that even if you've never used the Instant Pot® before, you can easily follow them.

How We Tested

Every recipe in this book was tested in a 6-litre Duo 7-in-1 Multi-Use Programmable Pressure Cooker. (Note that the size of Instant Pot® you use can affect the timings slightly. A larger pot will take slightly more time to come up to pressure, while a smaller one will take slightly less.)

The purpose of recipe testing is to make sure a recipe works every time you make it, that the timings are accurate, that it tastes great, and that the finished product is of the highest quality possible. We tested these recipes until we got the results we wanted: Perfectly cooked meats and poultry that were juicy, tender and never dried out. Vegetables that maintained their bright colours and fresh flavours, with an optimum texture that was appropriate to the dish – whether that was creamy and tender baby potatoes or barely cooked courgette that still had a bit of a bite. And fish and shellfish that came out of the cooker with their delicate textures and flavours intact.

Understanding the Timings

One of strongest advantages of the Instant Pot® – inherent in its name – is its ability to help you make fresh food fast. So the timings in the banners at the top of each recipe contain very important information. Here's how we define each term:

Prep Time: This refers to everything in the method that is done before the lid is secured on the pot and the button is selected for the first (and often only) closed-pot cooking function. That includes preparing and chopping fresh vegetables and browning and searing meats and poultry. Some recipes require a little bit of additional prep work while the pot is cooking – and if so, that time is included in the Total Time – but most don't, so you can walk away and do other things.

Function: This simply refers to which function(s) on the Instant Pot® is used to make that recipe and at which level it is used.

Closed Pot Time: This is important to note. It is not the cook time, which is specified in the recipe, but rather the entire time the lid is on the pot, which – in the case of pressure cooking – includes the time it takes for the pot to come up to pressure, cook and depressurise, whether by a natural or quick release. For slow cooking, it refers to the minimum cooking time given in the recipe.

Total Time: This refers to the Prep Time and Closed Pot Time totals, plus any additional steps that are not part of that (such as marinating, chilling, standing or simmering). Those are noted separately after a + sign in the Total Time box.

Reading the Recipes

The recipe method is broken down into three sections: Prep, Cook, and Serve.

Prep: See the 'Understanding the Timings' section, left, for a definition of Prep. This step always ends with securing the lid on the pot and either closing the pressure-release valve (for pressure-cooking and steaming) or opening the pressure-release valve (for slow-cooking and all other functions except sautéing, which is done with no lid).

Cook: This includes the selection of the cook function and, if pressure cooking, the type of release that should be used when cooking is complete. If there are a few additional cooking steps that follow, they are also included in this step.

Serve: This refers to the last steps in the method – often it is simply seasoning a dish, sprinkling it with fresh herbs or transferring it to a bowl or platter – that are done to get ready to serve the dish.

*Note: The recipes in this book refer to the steam rack that came with your Instant Pot® as 'the trivet'. This is to distinguish it from a collapsible basket-style vegetable steamer – both of which are used in these recipes. Sometimes just one is used; sometimes both. Particularly if your vegetable steamer doesn't have legs, it is helpful to stack it on top of the trivet in the pot to keep foods out of the water or other liquid at the bottom of the pot.

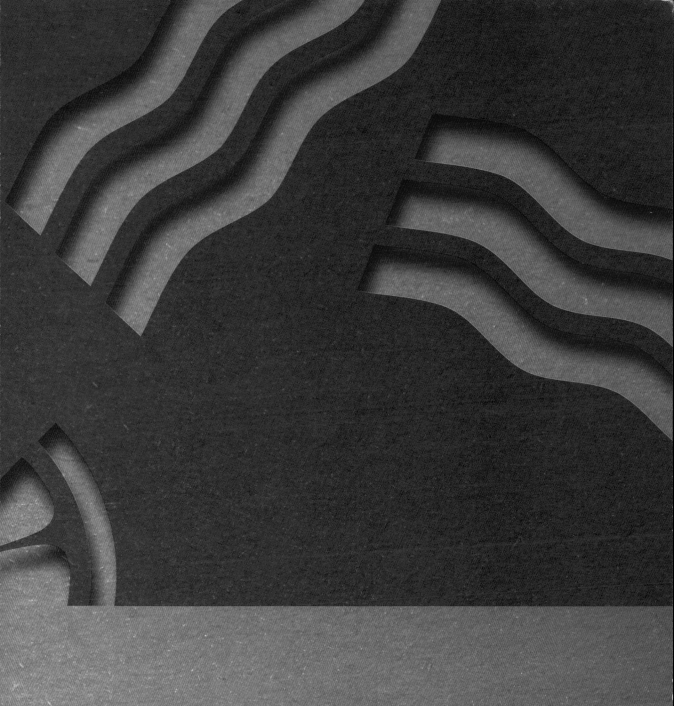

Breakfast

Chai-Spiced Breakfast Quinoa with Berries

Instead of getting your chai fix in a cup, try it in a bowl – in this healthy and nicely spiced grain-based breakfast dish. Fresh berries are stirred into the creamy grains and placed on top – with a drizzle of honey.

PREP TIME	FUNCTION	CLOSED POT TIME	TOTAL TIME
10 minutes	Slow Cook (More)	2 hours	2 hours 10 minutes

SERVES: 6

340 ml quinoa

1.2 litres water

90 g honey

1 tablespoon coconut oil

2 teaspoons minced fresh ginger

1 teaspoon ground cardamom

1 teaspoon ground cinnamon

¼ teaspoon ground cloves

¼ teaspoon ground nutmeg

¼ teaspoon salt

240 ml chilled coconut milk (full fat) or single cream

250 g raspberries, chopped strawberries, blueberries and/ or blackberries

Honey

PREP

Place quinoa in a sieve and rinse well under cool running water; let drain. Combine quinoa, the water, honey, coconut oil, ginger, cardamom, cinnamon, cloves, nutmeg and salt in the Instant Pot®. Secure the lid on the pot. Open the pressure-release valve.

COOK

Select **SLOW COOK** and adjust to **MORE**. Cook for 2 to 3 hours or until grains are tender. Press **CANCEL**.

SERVE

Stir in the coconut milk and 125 g of the fresh berries. Top each serving with the remaining berries and drizzle with honey.

Coconut-Lime Breakfast Porridge

Coconut and lime give this creamy breakfast cereal a tropical touch. Topped with fresh, juicy blackberries, it's a healthy, eye-opening way to start your day.

PREP TIME	FUNCTION	CLOSED POT TIME	TOTAL TIME	RELEASE
5 minutes	Porridge (Less)	30 minutes	35 minutes	Natural

SERVES: 3 to 4

Non-stick cooking spray

160 g porridge

240 ml chilled coconut milk

½ teaspoon finely grated lime zest

2 tablespoons freshly squeezed lime juice

1 tablespoon honey or agave nectar

475 ml cold water

⅛ teaspoon salt

250 g fresh blackberries, washed

PREP

Spray the inner pot of the Instant Pot® lightly with cooking spray (this helps reduce foaming and aids in cleanup). Combine the oats, coconut milk, lime zest, lime juice, honey, the water and salt in the pot. Stir well. Secure the lid on the pot. Close the pressure-release valve.

COOK

Select **PORRIDGE** and adjust to **LESS.** When cooking is complete, use a natural release to depressurise. Remove lid; set aside. Stir porridge well, allowing any excess liquid to be absorbed.

SERVE

Serve porridge in warm bowls topped with fresh blackberries.

Pumpkin-Spice Porridge Oats

The wildly popular pumpkin-spice combo infuses this hearty oatmeal flavoured with warm spices and maple syrup and studded with dried cranberries. Crunchy toasted nuts on top add texture and nutrition. Perfect for an autumn morning!

PREP TIME	FUNCTION	CLOSED POT TIME	TOTAL TIME	RELEASE
10 minutes	Pressure/Manual (High)	20 minutes	30 minutes	Natural

SERVES: 4

Non-stick cooking spray (optional)

530 ml water

240 ml unsweetened plain or vanilla almond, soy or cashew milk

Pinch of salt

½ teaspoon grated nutmeg

¼ teaspoon ground cardamom

1 to 2 cinnamon sticks

30 g dried cranberries

160 g porridge oats

110 g pumpkin puree or 75 g diced pumpkin or other squash

1 to 2 teaspoons pumpkin pie spice

Maple syrup

30 g chopped toasted pecans or walnuts

PREP

Spray the inner pot of the Instant Pot® lightly with cooking spray if desired (this helps reduce foaming and aids in cleanup). Combine the water and milk in the pot. Stir in the salt, nutmeg, cardamom, cinnamon sticks and cranberries. Add the oats and pumpkin, but do not stir. Secure the lid on the pot. Close the pressure-release valve.

COOK

Select **MANUAL** and cook at high pressure for 10 minutes. When cooking is complete, use a natural release to depressurise.

Carefully remove the lid, tilting it away from you.

SERVE

Stir the mixture. If it seems watery, place the lid back on and let sit 5 minutes. Open carefully. Use long tongs to remove and discard the cinnamon sticks. Add the pumpkin pie spice and maple syrup to taste.

Top each bowl with toasted nuts.

PUMPKIN-SPICE BUCKWHEAT: Make this dish with buckwheat groats instead of porridge oats. Follow the same directions.

Jill Nussinow blogs at TheVeggieQueen.com and is the author of *Vegan Under Pressure*.

Breakfast Sausage Meatballs with Maple-Apricot Glaze

Meatballs for breakfast? You bet! Especially when they're seasoned with classic breakfast-sausage herbs and spices, such as sage, mustard and caraway – and a hint of heat from cayenne. The sweetness of the apricots and maple syrup beautifully balances the savoury flavours.

PREP TIME	FUNCTION	CLOSED POT TIME	TOTAL TIME	RELEASE
55 minutes	Sauté (Less); Pressure/Manual (High)	20 minutes	1 hour 15 minutes	Quick

SERVES: 6

- 1 egg
- 1 medium cooking apple, peeled, cored and finely chopped
- 50 g quick-cooking oats
- 50 g thinly sliced spring onions
- 1 teaspoon dried sage, crushed
- ½ teaspoon salt
- ½ teaspoon ground mustard
- ¼ teaspoon caraway seeds or fennel seeds, finely crushed* (optional)
- ¼ teaspoon black pepper
- ⅛ to ¼ teaspoon cayenne pepper (optional)
- 450 g to 550 g minced turkey
- 1 to 2 tablespoons cooking oil
- 80 ml water
- 50 g chopped dried apricots
- 120 ml pure maple syrup
- 150 g apricot preserves

PREP

In a large bowl beat egg lightly. Stir in apple, oats, spirng onions, sage, salt, mustard, caraway seeds (if using), black pepper and cayenne pepper (if using). Add turkey; mix well.

Shape mixture into eighteen 5-cm meatballs. Select **SAUTÉ** on the Instant Pot® and adjust to **LESS**. Once hot, add 1 tablespoon of the oil. Cook meatballs, half at a time, in hot oil until meatballs are browned, carefully turning occasionally to lightly brown all sides evenly, for about 10 minutes. If necessary, add remaining oil to pot to prevent sticking. Transfer meatballs to a large plate when browned. Press **CANCEL**.

Add the water, apricots, syrup and preserves to pot. Stir until combined. Place the trivet in the bottom of the pot. Arrange browned meatballs on trivet, stacking as needed so all fit in the pot. Secure the lid on the pot. Close the pressure-release valve.

COOK

Select **MANUAL** and cook at high pressure for 6 minutes. When cooking is complete, use a quick release to depressurise.

SERVE

Transfer meatballs to a large shallow serving bowl. Remove trivet from pot. Stir sauce in bottom of pot. Pour over meatballs. Toss gently to coat meatballs with sauce. Serve warm.

*TIP: Use a spice grinder or clean coffee grinder to easily crush seeds.

Spinach, Tomato & Feta Frittatas

These individual frittatas are made in 170-g ramekins. To give the Greek flavour profile a boost, substitute dried oregano for the dried basil.

PREP TIME	FUNCTION		CLOSED POT TIME	TOTAL TIME	RELEASE
15 minutes	Pressure/Manual (High)		15 minutes	30 minutes	Quick

SERVES: 4

- 360 ml water
- Non-stick cooking spray
- 50 g chopped, seeded tomato
- 55 g coarsely chopped baby spinach
- 1 spring onion, sliced
- 30 g crumbled feta cheese, divided
- 4 eggs, beaten
- 1 tablespoon milk
- ¼ teaspoon dried basil, crushed
- ⅛ teaspoon salt
- Dash black pepper

PREP

Place the trivet–with handles under the rack–in the Instant Pot®. Add the water to pot.

Coat four 170-g ramekins with cooking spray. Divide tomato, spinach, spring onion and half of the feta cheese among the ramekins. In a small bowl combine eggs, milk, basil, salt and pepper. Pour egg mixture into ramekins. Cover each ramekin with foil. Arrange 3 of the ramekins evenly on the trivet. Set remaining ramekin on top of the other three.

Secure the lid on the pot. Close the pressure-release valve.

COOK

Select **MANUAL** and cook at high pressure for 5 minutes. When cooking is complete, use a quick release to depressurise.

SERVE

Carefully remove ramekins from pot. Remove foil and top with remaining feta cheese.

Crustless Tomato-Spinach Quiche

This veggie quiche is especially delicious when made with ripe, juicy summer tomatoes.

PREP TIME	FUNCTION	CLOSED POT TIME	TOTAL TIME	RELEASE
20 minutes	Pressure/Manual (High)	1 hour 15 minutes	1 hour 35 minutes	Natural

SERVES: 6

- **360** ml water
- **12** large eggs
- **120** ml milk
- **½** teaspoon salt
- **¼** teaspoon black pepper
- **150** g fresh baby spinach, roughly chopped (one 150g packet)
- **200** g diced, seeded tomato
- **3** large spring onions, sliced (green part only)
- **4** tomato slices
- **25** g grated Parmesan cheese

PREP
Place the trivet in the pot. Pour the water into the Instant Pot®.

In a large bowl whisk together the eggs, milk, salt and pepper. Add spinach, diced tomato and spring onions to egg mixture and stir to combine. Lightly grease a 1.5-litre baking dish. Transfer to prepared dish. Gently place sliced tomatoes on top and sprinkle with Parmesan cheese.

Cover top of dish with foil. Tear a 45-cm-long sheet of foil. Fold the sheet lengthwise into thirds to make a long, narrow sling. Use the sling to place the dish on the trivet in the pot. Secure the lid on the pot. Close the pressure-release valve.

COOK
Select **MANUAL** and cook at high pressure for 20 minutes. When cooking is complete, use a natural release to depressurise.

Carefully open the lid and lift out the dish.

SERVE
If desired, grill until top is lightly browned.

Barbara Schieving is the creator of the blog PressureCookingToday.com.

Eggs Shakshuka

Pronounced (shahk-SHOO-kah), this dish of eggs poached in rich, spicy tomato sauce (the degree of heat varies from recipe to recipe) is a popular breakfast in North Africa and the Middle East. The heat level of this version is fairly mild.

PREP TIME	FUNCTION	CLOSED POT TIME	TOTAL TIME	RELEASE
30 minutes	Sauté (Normal); Pressure/Manual (High, Low)	20 minutes	50 minutes	Quick

SERVES: 6

- 1 tablespoon olive oil
- 1 medium onion, chopped
- 1 clove garlic, minced
- 1 large red pepper, chopped
- 800 g diced ripe red tomatoes (4 to 6 medium tomatoes)
- 2 tablespoons tomato paste
- 1 teaspoon chilli powder
- 1½ teaspoons ground cumin
- 1 teaspoon sweet paprika
- ¼ teaspoon cayenne
- ½ teaspoon caraway seeds, crushed
- 6 eggs
- 170 g feta cheese, crumbled
- 50 g thinly sliced spinach leaves

PREP

Select **SAUTÉ** on the Instant Pot® and adjust to **NORMAL**. When hot, add the olive oil, onion and garlic. Cook and stir for 3 minutes or until onion is soft. Press **CANCEL**.

Add red pepper, tomatoes, tomato paste, chilli powder, cumin, paprika, cayenne and caraway. Stir to combine. Secure the lid on the pot. Close the pressure-release valve.

COOK

Select **MANUAL** and cook at high pressure for 5 minutes. When cooking is complete, use a quick release to depressurise.

Once steam is released, open lid. Working one egg at a time, break eggs on top of the hot sauce, spacing evenly.* Secure the lid on the pot. Close the pressure-release valve. Select **MANUAL** and cook at low pressure for 1 minute. When cooking is complete, use a quick release to depressurise.

SERVE

Using a large spoon, transfer eggs and sauce onto serving plates. Sprinkle each serving with feta cheese and sliced spinach; serve immediately.

*TIP: It's easiest to first crack each egg into a cup and gently pour it into the hot tomato sauce.

Bagel-Lox Strata

This elegant strata is perfect for entertaining company for brunch. Serve it with a crisp green salad, ripe tomato wedges or fresh fruit – and a little bit of something bubbly, if you'd like.

PREP TIME	FUNCTION	CLOSED POT TIME	TOTAL TIME	RELEASE
20 minutes	Pressure/Manual (High)	35 minutes	55 minutes	Quick

SERVES: 6

240 ml water

2 seeded bagels, cut into bite-size pieces

28 g cream cheese, cut into 1cm pieces

55 g thinly sliced smoked salmon (lox-style), cut into small pieces

2 tablespoons finely chopped onion

1 tablespoon snipped fresh chives

4 eggs

240 ml milk

110 g cottage cheese

2 teaspoons snipped fresh dill

PREP
Place the trivet in the bottom of the Instant Pot®. Add the water to the pot.

Lightly grease a 1.5-litre round ceramic or glass baking dish. Arrange half of the bagel pieces in the prepared dish. Top with cream cheese, salmon, onion and chives. Arrange the remaining bagel pieces over salmon mixture.

In a medium bowl combine eggs, milk, cottage cheese and dill. Pour evenly over ingredients in dish. Press lightly with the back of a large spoon to moisten all of the bagels. Cover with foil. Place the dish on the trivet. Secure the lid on the pot. Close the pressure-release valve.

COOK
Select **MANUAL** and cook at high pressure for 25 minutes. When cooking is complete, use a quick release to depressurise.

SERVE
Carefully remove the dish from the cooker. Uncover the dish. If desired, grill the strata 10 cm from the heat for 3 to 4 minutes or until the top is lightly browned.

Bacon & Egg Breakfast Bowl

The Instant Pot® makes quick work of porridge oats, but instead of the standard sweetened cereal, this recipe turns the oats into a savoury breakfast bowl topped with bacon and eggs.

PREP TIME	FUNCTION	CLOSED POT TIME	TOTAL TIME	RELEASE
15 minutes	Sauté (Normal); Porridge (Normal)	30 minutes	45 minutes	Natural

SERVES: 4

4	slices bacon, coarsely diced
75	g diced onion
2	garlic cloves, minced
80	g porridge oats
475	ml chicken stock
¼	teaspoon black pepper
⅛	teaspoon chilli flakes
4	eggs
	Salt and black pepper
1	avocado, sliced
	Snipped fresh chives

PREP

Select **SAUTÉ** on Instant Pot® and adjust to **NORMAL**. When hot, add the bacon and cook, stirring occasionally, until bacon is crisp. Remove bacon to a kitchen paper-lined plate. Press **CANCEL**. Remove all but 1 tablespoon of the grease from the pot, reserving extra grease in a small dish.

Select **SAUTÉ** and adjust to **NORMAL**. Add onion and garlic to pot. Cook, stirring, for 2 to 3 minutes or just until fragrant. Press **CANCEL**. Add oats, stock, black pepper and chilli flakes Secure the lid on the pot. Close the pressure-release valve.

COOK

Select **PORRIDGE** and adjust to **NORMAL**. Once cooking is complete, use a natural release to depressurise.

When pressure release is nearly complete, heat remaining bacon grease in a frying pan. Add eggs and cook 3 to 4 minutes or until whites are nearly set. Season with salt and black pepper to taste. Carefully flip, if desired, and cook for 1 to 3 minutes until desired doneness.

SERVE

Release any remaining steam from the pot by opening pressure-release valve. Divide oats among four bowls. Top with bacon, egg and avocado. Sprinkle with chives.

Cinnamon-Spiced Breakfast Bake with Bacon

Looking for something a little naughty and indulgent? This bread-pudding-style casserole is made with a combination of torn French bread and doughnuts and finished off with maple syrup and icing sugar. Smoky, salty bacon provides a nice contrast to all of that sweetness.

PREP TIME	FUNCTION	CLOSED POT TIME	TOTAL TIME	RELEASE
20 minutes	Sauté (Less); Pressure/Manual (High)	45 minutes	1 hour 5 minutes + 15 minutes	Quick

SERVES: 6

- 100 g French bread cubes (1-cm cubes)
- 200 g torn doughnuts (cinnamon sugar-dusted and/or glazed doughnuts)
- 6 eggs
- 475 ml semi-skimmed milk
- ¼ teaspoon pumpkin pie spice or ground cinnamon
- ¼ teaspoon salt
- 1 tablespoon pure vanilla extract
- 4 slices bacon, diced
- Non-stick cooking spray
- 475 ml water
- Pure maple syrup
- Icing sugar

PREP

Combine bread cubes and torn doughnuts in a large bowl. Whisk together eggs, milk, pumpkin pie spice, salt and vanilla in a mixing bowl. Pour over bread and doughnuts. Stir to combine; set aside.

Select **SAUTÉ** on the Instant Pot® and adjust to **LESS**. Sauté diced bacon for 5 minutes. Press **CANCEL**. Remove bacon pieces to a kitchen-paper-lined plate. Drain grease and wipe pot clean with kitchen paper.

Stir bacon into doughnut and egg mixture. Pour into a 1.5–1.9-litre soufflé dish coated with cooking spray. Cover with foil. Add water to pot. Place soufflé dish in the pot. Secure the lid on the pot. Close the pressure-release valve.

COOK

Select **MANUAL** and cook at high pressure for 35 minutes. When cooking is complete, use a quick release to depressurise. Remove foil and let stand for 15 minutes before serving.

SERVE

Spoon into serving bowls. Drizzle with maple syrup and icing sugar.

Hearty Eggs Benedict Breakfast Casserole

This breakfast casserole has all of the flavours of traditional Eggs Benedict without the egg poaching – and with a healthy dose of veggies.

PREP TIME	FUNCTION	CLOSED POT TIME	TOTAL TIME	RELEASE
30 minutes	Sauté (Normal); Pressure/Manual (High)	30 minutes	1 hour + 20 minutes bake/	Quick

SERVES: 6

- 1 tablespoon olive oil
- 75 g sliced fresh button mushrooms
- 85 g chopped red sweet pepper
- 3 pring onions
- 5 eggs
- 285 ml whole milk
- ¼ teaspoon black pepper
- 4 muffins, split and toasted
- 170 g thinly sliced back bacon or cooked ham, chopped
- 360 ml water

MOCK HOLLANDAISE SAUCE

- 75 g soured cream
- 75 g mayonnaise
- 2 teaspoons lemon juice
- 2 teaspoons Dijon mustard
  Milk (optional)
  Sliced spring onion (optional)

PREP

Select **SAUTÉ** on the Instant Pot® and adjust to **NORMAL**. When hot, add oil, mushrooms and red pepper. Cook for 5 minutes, stirring occasionally. Thinly slice spring onions, keeping white bottoms separate from green tops. Add white parts of spring onions to pot with vegetables. Cook for 2 minutes more, stirring occasionally. Press **CANCEL**.

Meanwhile, in a large bowl whisk together eggs, milk and black pepper. Cut or tear toasted muffins into 2.5-cm pieces. Add to milk mixture. Stir in bacon. Add vegetables from the pot along with sliced spring onion tops and bacon. Stir to combine.

Transfer bread mixture to a greased 1.5-litre round ceramic or glass casserole (make sure the dish will fit in the Instant Pot® first). Spread to an even layer. Cover top with foil. Tear a 45-cm-long sheet of foil. Fold the sheet lengthwise into thirds to make a long, narrow sling.

Place the trivet in the bottom of the pot. Add the water to the pot. Place filled casserole in the centre of the foil sling. Use the sling to lower the casserole into the pot until it sits on the steam rack. Tuck foil into pot so the lid will fit. Secure the lid on the pot. Close the pressure-release valve.

COOK

Select **MANUAL** and cook at high pressure for 20 minutes. When cooking is complete, use a quick release to depressurise.

SERVE

Lift the casserole out of the pot using the foil sling. Uncover casserole. Bake casserole in a 200°C/400°F oven for 10 to 15 minutes or until top is browned. Let casserole stand 10 minutes before serving.

Meanwhile, for Mock Hollandaise Sauce, combine soured cream, mayonnaise, lemon juice and mustard in a small saucepan. Cook and stir over medium-low heat until warm. If desired, stir in a little milk to thin. If desired, stir in sliced spring onion. Drizzle sauce over each serving.

Three-Cheese Bacon-Spring-Onion Crustless Quiche

Cheddar, Parmesan and blue cheese add tanginess and rich flavour to this yummy quiche. Substitute smoked paprika for the regular paprika if you like.

PREP TIME	FUNCTION	CLOSED POT TIME	TOTAL TIME	RELEASE
15 minutes	Pressure/Manual (High)	40 minutes	55 minutes + 10 minutes stand	Natural

SERVES: 4 to 6

- 360 ml water
- 6 eggs
- 175 ml milk
- 50 g thinly sliced spring onions
- 55 g grated sharp cheddar cheese
- 30 g crumbled blue cheese
- 6 slices bacon, cooked until crisp and crumbled
- 3 tablespoons grated Parmesan cheese
- ½ teaspoon freshly ground black pepper
- ¼ teaspoon to ½ teaspoon paprika
- Sliced spring onions

PREP

Place the trivet in the pot. Add the water to Instant Pot®. Grease a 950-ml soufflé dish.

In a medium bowl whisk together eggs, milk, spring onions, cheddar cheese, blue cheese, bacon, 2 tablespoons of the Parmesan cheese and the pepper. Pour into prepared dish. Sprinkle with the remaining 1 tablespoon Parmesan cheese and the paprika. Cover dish with foil. Place covered dish on trivet. Secure the lid on the pot. Close the pressure-release valve.

COOK

Select **MANUAL** and cook at high pressure for 20 minutes. When cooking is complete, use a natural release to depressurise.

SERVE

Let cool for at least 10 minutes before serving. Sprinkle with additional sliced spring onions just before serving.

Appetisers & Snacks

Savoury Blue Cheese Appetiser Cheesecake

With a crust of crushed buttery crackers and chopped pecans, this savoury cheesecake takes the standard cheeseball to a new level. Paired with crisp, sweet slices of apple and pear, it's perfect for an autumn party.

PREP TIME	FUNCTION	CLOSED POT TIME	TOTAL TIME	RELEASE
45 minutes	Manual/Pressure (High)	1 hour 5 minutes	1 hour 50 minutes + 1 hour cool + 4 hours chill	Natural

SERVES: 12

Non-stick cooking spray

175 g finely crushed buttery crackers

60 g finely chopped pecans

3 tablespoons melted butter

450 g cream cheese, softened

115 g blue cheese, crumbled

60 ml double cream

1 teaspoon dried basil

½ teaspoon garlic powder

¼ teaspoon ground white pepper

3 eggs, room temperature

25 g diced spring onions

475 ml water

Crackers or crostini and pear and/or apple slices, for serving

PREP

Lightly spray a 15-cm or 18-cm springform tin with cooking spray. Cut a piece of baking paper to fit the bottom of the tin. Place in the tin and spray again; set aside.

Combine crackers, pecans and butter; mix well. Press into bottom and about 4 cm up the sides of the springform tin.

Beat cream cheese, blue cheese and cream in a large bowl until smooth and creamy. Beat in basil, garlic powder and white pepper. Add eggs, one at a time, beating just until egg is combined. Fold in spring onions. Pour into prepared crust. (Tin will be full.) Tent with foil.

Place trivet in the bottom of the pot. Pour the water into the Instant Pot®. Cut a piece of foil the same size as a piece of kitchen paper. Place the foil under the kitchen paper and place the tin on top of the kitchen paper. Wrap the bottom of the tin in the foil with the kitchen paper as a barrier.

Fold a 45-cm-long piece of foil into thirds lengthwise. Place under the tin and use the two sides as a sling to place cheesecake on the trivet in the pot. Secure the lid on the pot. Close the pressure-release valve.

COOK

Select **MANUAL** and cook at high pressure for 40 minutes. When cooking is complete, use a natural release to depressurise.

SERVE

Remove the cheesecake from the pot using the sling. Cool on the rack for 1 hour and chill for at least 4 hours. Carefully remove tin sides.

Serve cheesecake with crackers or crostini and pear and/or apple slices.

Greek Stuffed Vine Leaves

These delicate parcels of lamb or beef and rice flavoured with lemon, parsley, mint and dill – called dolmades – are a classic Greek *meze*, or appetiser. Boiling the leaves before filling and cooking tenderises them.

PREP TIME	FUNCTION		CLOSED POT TIME	TOTAL TIME	RELEASE
45 minutes	Pressure/Manual (High)		40 minutes	1 hour 25 minutes	Natural

SERVES: about 34

- 450 g minced lamb or beef
- 400 g uncooked easy-cook rice
- 3 tablespoons fresh lemon juice
- 2 tablespoons finely chopped fresh flat-leaf parsley
- 2 tablespoons finely chopped fresh mint
- 2 tablespoons finely chopped fresh dill
- 2 tablespoons finely chopped spring onions
- 1 teaspoon salt
- 1 425-g to 450-g jar vine leaves (about 30 to 36 leaves)
- 120 ml water
- 120 ml lemon juice
- Plain Greek yogurt (optional)

PREP

To make the filling, in a large bowl combine lamb, rice, the 3 tablespoons lemon juice, parsley, mint, dill, spring onions and salt; set aside.

Bring a large pan of water to a boil. Add vine leaves. Boil for 5 minutes. Drain well.

To assemble the stuffed vine leaves, place four to six whole vine leaves at a time on a work surface with the stem sides up and stem ends pointing towards you. Pinch or trim off any long or tough stems. Depending on the size of the leaf, shape 1 to 2 tablespoons of the filling into a 4-cm to 5-cm log and place it on the leaf perpendicular to the stem end. Roll the end of the leaf over the filling, tuck in the sides and roll tightly into a cigar shape. Repeat with remaining vine leaves and filling.

Place the rolled vine leaves in the Instant Pot®, packing them together tightly and keeping them in the same direction. Once you finish a layer, turn the second layer of vine leaves in the opposite direction. After all the vine leaves are packed into the pot, add the water and the 120ml lemon juice to the pot. Secure the lid on the pot. Close the pressure-release valve.

COOK

Select **MANUAL** and cook at high pressure for 15 minutes. When cooking is complete, use a natural release to depressurise.

SERVE

Serve stuffed vine leaves warm. If desired, serve yogurt for dipping. (They can also be chilled and served cold.)

Asian Chicken Sliders with Pickled Cucumbers & Onions

This slider features the famous Asian flavour quartet – sweet, sour, salt and heat – but the flavours are subtle enough to appeal to both kids and adults.

PREP TIME	FUNCTION	CLOSED POT TIME	TOTAL TIME	RELEASE
45 minutes	Sauté (Normal); Pressure/Manual (High)	15 minutes	1 hour	Quick

SERVES: 12

SRIRACHA MAYONNAISE

110 g mayonnaise

2 to 3 teaspoons sriracha sauce

PICKLED CUCUMBERS

150 g thinly sliced cucumber

130 g thinly sliced red onion

60 ml rice vinegar (unseasoned)

2 teaspoons sugar

¼ teaspoon chilli flakes

SLIDERS

450 g minced chicken breast

40 g panko breadcrumbs

25 g sliced spring onions

1 egg, slightly beaten

1 tablespoon tamari sauce

1 tablespoon sriracha

2 teaspoons black bean garlic sauce

¼ teaspoon salt

1 tablespoon vegetable or olive oil

240 ml reduced-salt chicken stock or water

12 burger buns

PREP

For the mayonnaise, stir together mayonnaise and desired amount of sriracha. Chill until ready to use.

For the pickled cucumbers, combine cucumber, red onion, vinegar, sugar and chilli flakes in a bowl. Chill until ready to use.

For the sliders, place chicken, breadcrumbs and spring onions in a large bowl. Add beaten egg, tamari, sriracha, black bean sauce and salt to chicken. Mix thoroughly to combine. Using wet hands (to keep the mixture from sticking), divide and shape into 12 equal-size meatballs, about 4 cm in diameter.

Select **SAUTÉ** on the Instant Pot® and adjust to **NORMAL**. Add 1 tablespoon oil. When hot, cook half of the meatballs until browned on all sides, carefully turning, for about 6 minutes. Remove browned meatballs and repeat with remaining half. Return all meatballs to pot. Press **CANCEL**. Add stock. Secure the lid on the pot. Close the pressure-release valve.

COOK

Select **MANUAL** and cook at for 5 minutes on high pressure. When cooking is complete, use a quick release to depressurise.

SERVE

Remove meatballs from pot using a slotted spoon. For each slider, spread about 2 teaspoons sriracha mayonnaise on each bottom bun. Top each with a meatball and pickled cucumbers. Add bun tops and serve.

Italian Cocktail Meatballs

There aren't too many non-vegetarians who don't love a good meatball – whether it's served with sauce and spaghetti for dinner or as an appetiser on the end of a cocktail stick.

PREP TIME	FUNCTION	CLOSED POT TIME	TOTAL TIME	RELEASE
45 minutes	Sauté (Normal); Pressure/Manual (High)	20 minutes	1 hour 5 minutes	Quick

SERVES: 10 to 12

MEATBALLS

- 1 **egg**
- 35 g **fine dry breadcrumbs**
- 25 g **finely grated Parmesan cheese**
- 2 **tablespoons milk**
- 1 **tablespoon chopped fresh basil**
- 1 **tablespoon chopped fresh flat-leaf parsley**
- 2 **cloves garlic, minced**
- ½ **teaspoon salt**
- ¼ **teaspoon black pepper**
- 450 g **minced beef**
  Finely grated Parmesan (optional)

SAUCE

- 1 **tablespoon olive oil**
- 110 g **chopped onion**
- ¼ **teaspoon salt**
- ¼ **teaspoon chilli flakes**
- 2 **cloves garlic, minced**
- 1 **800-g tin crushed tomatoes**
- 1 **230-g tin tomato sauce**
- 2 **tablespoons chopped fresh basil**

PREP

For the meatballs, in a medium bowl beat egg with a fork. Stir in breadcrumbs, Parmesan, milk, basil, parsley, garlic, salt and black pepper. Add minced beef; mix well. Shape mixture into 4-cm meatballs.

For the sauce, select **SAUTÉ** on the Instant Pot® and adjust to **NORMAL**. Heat oil in pot; add onion, salt and chilli flakes and cook for 2 to 3 minutes or until softened, stirring frequently. Add garlic; cook and stir 1 minute more. Press **CANCEL**. Add crushed tomatoes and tomato sauce; stir well. Add meatballs to sauce. Secure the lid on the pot. Close the pressure-release valve.

COOK

Select **MANUAL** and cook at high pressure for 6 minutes. When cooking is complete, use a quick release to depressurise.

SERVE

Stir basil into sauce and meatball mixture. If desired, top with additional Parmesan cheese.

Artichoke Dip

There is some version of this delicious dip at nearly any gathering. This one incorporates white beans into the mix and swaps low-fat yogurt for the usual soured cream and mayonnaise. It's every bit as flavourful as the standard stuff – and lots better for you.

PREP TIME	FUNCTION	CLOSED POT TIME	TOTAL TIME	RELEASE
10 minutes	Pressure/Manual (High)	45 minutes	55 minutes	Natural

SERVES: 16 (50-g servings)

- 100 g dried cannellini beans, soaked overnight or quick-soaked
- 240 ml water
- 2 800-g tins artichoke hearts, drained
- 2 cloves garlic, smashed
- 170 g plain low-fat yogurt
- 1 teaspoon salt, or to taste
- ¼ teaspoon black pepper
- 75 g grated Parmigiano Reggiano cheese
- Crostini and/or bagel chips

PREP
Place beans, the water and artichoke hearts in the Instant Pot®. Secure the lid on the pot. Close the pressure-release valve.

COOK
Select **MANUAL** and cook at high pressure for 25 minutes. When cooking is complete, use a natural release to depressurise.

SERVE
Add the garlic, yogurt, salt, pepper and cheese to the pot. Blend with an immersion blender.

Serve warm with crostini and/or bagel chips or chill tightly covered and remove from fridge 30 minutes before serving. The dip can be frozen up to 3 months.

Laura Pazzaglia is the creator of the blog HipPressureCooking.com.

Green Chilli Chicken Dip

This decadent blend of cream cheese and Monterey Jack is spiked with Mexican seasonings and salsa verde. Choose a salsa that fits your personal tolerance for heat. Either fire-roasted or regular salsa works just fine.

PREP TIME	FUNCTION	CLOSED POT TIME	TOTAL TIME
20 minutes	Sauté (Normal); Slow Cook (More)	2 hours	2 hours 20 minutes

SERVES: 24 to 32

- 1 tablespoon olive oil
- 75 g chopped onion
- 1 medium padrón pepper, seeded and chopped
- 2 cloves garlic, minced
- 375 g chopped cooked chicken
- 1 450-g jar salsa verde tomatillo salsa
- 1 225-g packet cream cheese, cubed
- 230 g grated Monterey Jack cheese
- 1 teaspoon chilli powder
- ½ teaspoon ground cumin
- 225 g soured cream
- 2 tablespoons chopped fresh coriander
- Diced tomato (optional)
- Sliced jalapeño pepper (optional)
- Tortilla chips, for serving

PREP

Select **SAUTÉ** on the Instant Pot® and adjust to **NORMAL**. Heat oil in pot. Add the onion and poblano. Cook for 3 to 5 minutes or until softened, stirring frequently. Add the garlic. Cook and stir for 1 minute more. Press **CANCEL**.

Add chicken, salsa, cream cheese, grated cheese, chilli powder and cumin. Secure the lid on the pot. Open the pressure-release valve.

COOK

Select **SLOW COOK** and adjust to **MORE**. Cook for 2 to 2½ hours, until heated through and cheese is melted; stir well to combine.

SERVE

Stir in soured cream and coriander. Press **CANCEL**.

If desired, garnish with diced tomato and sliced jalapeño. Serve with tortilla chips.

Buffalo Chicken Wings with Blue Cheese Dressing

Whip up a batch of these before watching a game with friends, or – because they're so fast and easy – simply because you're craving that irresistible combination of vinegary, spicy chicken cooled down with creamy blue cheese dressing and crunchy veggies.

PREP TIME	FUNCTION	CLOSED POT TIME	TOTAL TIME	RELEASE
20 minutes	Pressure/Manual (High)	25 minutes	45 minutes + 10 minutes grill	Quick

SERVES: 12 to 16

240 ml water

1.3 kg chicken wing pieces*

115 g unsalted butter

120 ml hot pepper sauce

1 tablespoon apple cider vinegar

¼ teaspoon Worcestershire sauce

¼ teaspoon cayenne pepper

¼ teaspoon garlic powder

Blue cheese dressing

Celery and carrot sticks

PREP

Place the trivet in the Instant Pot®. Add the water to pot. Add the chicken to the pot. Secure the lid on the pot. Close the pressure-release valve.

COOK

Select **MANUAL** and cook at high pressure for 10 minutes. When cooking is complete, use a quick release to depressurise.

Meanwhile, for the sauce, in a microwave-safe bowl melt the butter. Stir in the hot sauce, vinegar, Worcestershire sauce, cayenne and garlic powder.

Place the oven rack about 13 cm from the heat source. Preheat the grill. Line a large baking tin with foil. Using tongs, arrange the wings in a single layer on the baking tin. Pat the wings dry with kitchen paper. Brush the wings with half the sauce. Grill the wings for 5 minutes. Brush with remaining sauce and grill 5 minutes more or until wings are lightly browned.

SERVE

Serve the wings with blue cheese dressing and carrot and celery sticks.

*TIP: Or purchase 1.6 kg chicken wings and cut at the joint to make about 36 pieces.

Sesame-Chilli Edamame

Steaming edamame in the Instant Pot® is an ideal way to cook them. The pods get tender enough so you can easily strip them directly into your mouth with your teeth (yes, the proper way to eat edamame), but the beans retain an appealing crisp-tender bite. (Discard the pods.)

PREP TIME	FUNCTION	CLOSED POT TIME	TOTAL TIME	RELEASE
5 minutes	Steam	20 minutes	25 minutes	Quick

SERVES: 4 to 6

240 ml water

450 to 550 g frozen edamame
   (in shells)

1 tablespoon thinly sliced fresh
   chives

2 teaspoons toasted sesame oil

2 teaspoons sesame seeds, plus
   extra to serve

1 teaspoon flaked sea salt

½ teaspoon chilli flakes

½ teaspoon garlic powder

¼ teaspoon black pepper

PREP
Place a vegetable steamer basket in the Instant Pot®; add the water to pot. Place the edamame in the steamer basket. Secure the lid on the pot. Close the pressure-release valve.

COOK
Select **STEAM** and cook for 2 minutes. When cooking is complete, use a quick release to depressurise.

SERVE
Meanwhile, in a small bowl combine the chives, oil, sesame seeds, sea salt, chilli flakes, garlic powder and black pepper. Lift out the steamer basket, allowing excess water to drip away. Transfer edamame to a bowl. Toss with sesame oil. Sprinkle with spice mixture; toss gently to coat evenly.

Beef, Pork & Lamb

Kitchen-Sink Pot Roast

This dish features the simple, satisfying flavours of an old-school pot roast with a modern touch – a few handfuls of baby kale tossed in at the end for a splash of bright colour and a nutritional boost.

PREP TIME	FUNCTION	CLOSED POT TIME	TOTAL TIME	RELEASE
35 minutes	Sauté (Normal); Pressure/Manual (High)	1 hour 30 minutes	2 hours 5 minutes	Quick

SERVES: 6 to 8

- 1 1.6-kg to 1.8-kg boneless beef rump roast
- 1 teaspoon salt
- 1 teaspoon dried thyme
- ½ teaspoon black pepper
- 2 tablespoons vegetable oil
- 360 ml beef stock
- 240 ml dry red wine
- 4 medium Yukon gold potatoes, halved (unpeeled)
- 2 medium onions, quartered
- 4 large carrots, cut into 5-cm lengths
- 4 stalks celery, cut into 5-cm lengths
- 270 g baby kale

PREP

Season roast with salt, thyme and pepper. Select **SAUTÉ** on the Instant Pot® and adjust to **NORMAL**. When hot, add oil to the pot. Add the roast to the pot and brown on all sides for about 10 minutes. Press **CANCEL**. Add the stock and wine to the pot. Secure the lid on the pot. Close the pressure-release valve.

COOK

Select **MANUAL** and cook at high pressure for 50 minutes. When cooking time is complete, use a quick release to depressurise. Add the potatoes, onions, carrots and celery. Secure the lid on the pot. Close the pressure-release valve. Select **MANUAL** and cook at high pressure for 10 minutes. When cooking time is complete, use a quick release to depressurise.

SERVE

Remove vegetables and meat to a serving platter. Stir kale into hot juices in cooker and allow to just wilt for 1 to 2 minutes. Remove with a slotted spoon and transfer to platter. Spoon some of the juices over meat and vegetables.

Beef Shank Osso Buco with Citrus Gremolata

Traditional osso buco is made with veal shanks. This version takes a tougher cut of meat – bone-in beef shanks – and turns them meltingly tender. A sprinkle of gremolata – a blend of lemon, orange, garlic and parsley – right before serving gives the finished dish bright, fresh flavour.

PREP TIME	FUNCTION	CLOSED POT TIME	TOTAL TIME
45 minutes	Sauté (Normal); Slow Cook (More)	6 hours	6 hours 45 minutes

SERVES: 4

- 60 g plain flour
- 1 teaspoon salt
- ½ teaspoon freshly ground black pepper
- 4 bone-in beef shanks (1.1–1.3 kg)
- 2 tablespoons olive oil
- 150 g chopped onion
- 150 g chopped carrots
- 50 g chopped celery
- 4 cloves garlic, minced
- 55 g tomato paste
- 80 ml dry white wine
- ½ teaspoon dried marjoram
- ½ teaspoon dried thyme
- 285 ml beef stock
- 1 tablespoon balsamic vinegar
- 2 bay leaves
- Citrus Gremolata
- Cooked polenta (optional)

PREP

In a shallow dish combine flour, salt and pepper. Mix well. Dredge beef shanks in flour mixture, coating well.

Select **SAUTÉ** on the Instant Pot® and adjust to **NORMAL**. Add olive oil. Brown beef shanks in hot oil, one shank at a time, adding additional oil as needed. Set aside. Add onion, carrots and celery. Cook and stir vegetables for 5 to 6 minutes or until onions are tender. Stir in garlic, tomato paste and wine. Stir, scraping up any browned bits in bottom of pot. Press **CANCEL**. Arrange beef shanks on top of vegetables; sprinkle with marjoram and thyme. Add stock, vinegar and bay leaves. Secure the lid on the pot. Open the pressure-release valve.

COOK

Select **SLOW COOK** and adjust to **MORE**. Cook for 6 to 7 hours or until beef is fork tender. Press **CANCEL**.

When cooking is complete, transfer beef shanks to an oven-safe dish; cover with foil and keep warm in a 200°C/400°F oven. Remove and discard bay leaves. Skim excess fat from sauce.

SERVE

If desired, serve beef shanks over polenta. Spoon sauce over beef shanks. Sprinkle with Citrus Gremolata. Serve immediately.

CITRUS GREMOLATA: Combine the finely shredded zest of 2 lemons, the finely shredded zest of 1 orange, 1 tablespoon minced garlic and 30 g finely chopped fresh flat-leaf parsley. Mix well. May be prepared up to 2 days ahead when tightly covered and kept in the fridge.

Barbacoa-Style Shredded Beef

Although *barbacoa* has traditionally referred to meat that is slow-cooked over an open fire or in a hole in the ground above hot coals, this version is inspired by some contemporary Mexican interpretations that call for steaming. The results are the same – tender, juicy, highly seasoned meat. Serve with tortillas or rice.

PREP TIME	FUNCTION	CLOSED POT TIME	TOTAL TIME
45 minutes	Sauté (Normal); Slow Cook (More)	5 hours	5 hours 45 minutes

SERVES: 8

- 1 **1.1-kg to 1.25-kg beef braising steak**
- 2 **teaspoons paprika**
- 1½ **teaspoons dried oregano, crushed**
- 1½ **teaspoons ground cumin**
- 1 **teaspoon salt**
- ½ **teaspoon black pepper**
- ¼ **teaspoon ground cloves**
- 1 **tablespoon cooking oil**
- 120 **ml reduced-salt beef stock**
- 1 **medium onion, cut into wedges**
- 1 **tinned chipotle pepper in adobo sauce + 1 tablespoon adobo sauce from tin**
- 4 **cloves garlic, minced**
- 1 **bay leaf**
- 1 **230-g tin tomato passata**
- 60 **ml cider vinegar**
- 1 **tablespoon honey**
- 16 **corn tortillas, warmed**
  - **Salsa**
  - **Chopped avocado**
  - **Pickled Red Onion Slivers**
  - **Chopped fresh coriander**
  - **Lime wedges**

PREP
Trim fat from beef; cut beef into four portions. In a small bowl combine paprika, oregano, cumin, salt, black pepper and cloves. Sprinkle over all sides of beef portions, rubbing in with your fingers. Select **SAUTÉ** on the Instant Pot® and adjust heat to **NORMAL**. When hot, add oil and beef pieces, half at a time if needed. Brown beef portions, turning to brown all sides evenly, for about 10 minutes. Press **CANCEL**. Add beef stock, onion, chipotle pepper and adobo sauce, garlic and bay leaf to pot with beef. Secure the lid on the pot. Open the pressure-release valve.

COOK
Select **SLOW COOK** and adjust to **MORE**. Cook for 5 to 6 hours or until meat is tender. Press **CANCEL**.

SERVE
Transfer meat to a cutting board using a slotted spoon; cover to keep warm. Remove bay leaf from cooking juices and discard. Skim fat from top of cooking juices. Add passata, vinegar and honey to cooking juices in pot. Use an immersion blender* to blend cooking juices until very smooth.

Using two forks, shred the cooked beef. Add beef back to pot with cooking juices. Toss to coat meat with juices. Using a slotted spoon, serve meat in tortillas topped with salsa, avocado, Pickled Red Onion Slivers and coriander. Serve with lime wedges for squeezing.

PICKLED RED ONION SLIVERS: In a medium bowl combine 50 g slivered red onion and 80ml lime juice. Toss to coat; press down on onion to cover as much with the juice as possible. Cover; let stand at room temperature for 30 minutes or chill for up to 3 days, stirring occasionally. Drain onion to serve.

*If you don't have an immersion blender, transfer the cooking juices to a regular blender; cover and blend until smooth. Return blended juice to the pot.

Korean Beef Tacos with Sriracha Slaw

It was a beautiful day when someone decided to fuse the Korean seasonings for beef – soy, sugar, garlic, sesame and hot chiles – with the Mexican habit of enjoying cooked meat wrapped in a tortilla.

PREP TIME	FUNCTION	CLOSED POT TIME	TOTAL TIME
20 minutes	Sauté (Normal); Slow Cook (More)	6 hours	6 hours 20 minutes

SERVES: 8

BEEF

- 1 tablespoon vegetable oil
- 900 g to 1.1 kg boneless beef braising steak, cut into 3 to 4 chunks
- 1 Asian or regular pear, cored
- 60 ml reduced-salt soy sauce
- 3 tablespoons brown sugar
- 4½ teaspoons minced garlic
- 1 tablespoon sesame oil
- Dash cayenne pepper
- 1 tablespoon sesame seeds, toasted
- 16 15-cm flour tortillas
- Fresh coriander

SRIRACHA SLAW

- 55 g mayonnaise
- 2 teaspoons sriracha sauce
- 1 bag (400 g to 450 g) coleslaw mix

PREP

Select **SAUTÉ** on the Instant Pot® and adjust to **NORMAL**. Add oil to pot. When hot, add the chunks of beef and cook for 5 to 8 minutes or until well browned. Drain fat.

Shred pear into a medium bowl. Add soy sauce, brown sugar, garlic, sesame oil and cayenne pepper. Mix well. Pour over the beef. Press **CANCEL**. Secure the lid on the pot. Open the pressure-release valve.

COOK

Select **SLOW COOK** and adjust to **MORE**. Cook for 6 to 7 hours until beef is very tender. Press **CANCEL**.

SERVE

Combine mayonnaise and sriracha in a large bowl. Add coleslaw mix and toss to coat. Chill until beef is ready. Shred beef with two forks. Sprinkle with sesame seeds.

Portion beef into tortillas and top with slaw and coriander.

Philly-Cheese French Dip Sandwiches

This sandwich takes the classic Philly favourite of juicy, slow-cooked beef served on a crusty roll with peppers and melted cheese and makes it even better with the flavourful 'jus' served with French dips.

PREP TIME	FUNCTION	CLOSED POT TIME	TOTAL TIME
40 minutes	Sauté (Normal/More); Slow Cook (More)	5 hours 30 minutes	6 hours 10 minutes + 10 minutes rest

SERVES: 8

- 2 teaspoons onion powder
- 2 teaspoons garlic powder
- 3 teaspoons Italian seasoning
- 1 teaspoon salt
- 1 teaspoon black pepper
- 1 1.3-kg to 1.8-kg beef rump
- 2 to 3 tablespoons olive oil
- 2 onions, thinly sliced
- 2 green peppers, thinly sliced
- 120 ml red wine
- 1 430 ml carton beef stock
- 2 tablespoons Worcestershire sauce
- Panini buns
- Butter
- Sliced provolone cheese

PREP

In a small bowl combine onion powder, garlic powder, Italian seasoning, salt and black pepper. Rub spice mixture all over the beef.

Select **SAUTÉ** on the Instant Pot® and adjust to **NORMAL**. Add 2 tablespoons of the olive oil to the pot. When the oil is hot, place beef in the pot. Brown until deep brown on all sides for about 15 minutes. Remove roast and add the onions and the remaining 1 tablespoon olive oil. Cook the onions until softened and lightly browned, stirring occasionally, for about 5 minutes. Stir in peppers; cook for 1 minute. Add red wine; scrape up any browned bits in the pan. Press **CANCEL**. Select **SAUTÉ** and adjust to **MORE**. Add beef stock and Worcestershire sauce. Bring to boiling. Simmer for 10 minutes or until reduced by almost half. Press **CANCEL**.

Return the beef to the pot. Secure the lid on the pot. Open the pressure-release valve.

COOK

Select **SLOW COOK** and adjust to **MORE**. Cook for 5½ to 6 hours or until meat is tender. Press **CANCEL**.

SERVE

Transfer beef to a cutting board. Let rest for 10 minutes. Slice the meat. Use a slotted spoon to transfer the peppers and onions to a bowl.

Meanwhile, preheat oven to 220°C/425°F. Spread buns with butter. Arrange bun halves on a baking sheet, buttered sides up. Bake for 10 minutes or until lightly toasted.

Layer beef, the peppers, onions and provolone cheese onto the bottoms of the rolls. Bake for about 5 minutes more or until cheese is melted. Serve sandwiches with the juices left in the pot for dipping.

Asian Short Rib Noodle Bowl

Short ribs are ideal for the Instant Pot®–whether they're slow-cooked, as they are here–or are cooked under pressure. Either way, this tough cut turns so tender it literally falls off the bone. In this case, that's into a flavourful stock bursting with chewy udon noodles and sweet, crisp sugar snap peas.

PREP TIME	FUNCTION	CLOSED POT TIME	TOTAL TIME
30 minutes	Slow Cook (More); Sauté (Normal)	5 hours + 1 hour marinate	6 hours 30 minutes

SERVES: 8

- 175 ml reduced-salt soy sauce
- 710 ml low-salt beef stock
- 3 tablespoons sugar
- 1 teaspoon salt
- 3 tablespoons minced garlic
- 2 tablespoons minced fresh ginger
- 2 tablespoons toasted sesame oil
- 3 tablespoons minced spring onion
- ½ teaspoon chilli flakes
- 2.25 kg beef short ribs (8 ribs)
- 300 g fresh sugar snap peas
- 1 400-g packet (or two 200-g pouches) ready-to-serve udon stir-fry noodles

  Sesame seeds (optional)

  Sliced spring onions (optional)

PREP

In a large non-metallic container or large resealable plastic bag, combine soy sauce, beef stock, sugar, salt, garlic, ginger, sesame oil, minced spring onion, and chilli flakes. Mix until sugar dissolves. Add short ribs, pressing to fully immerse ribs in marinade. Let ribs marinate for 1 hour at room temperature or in the fridge overnight.

Transfer ribs and marinade to Instant Pot®. Secure the lid on the pot. Open the pressure-release valve.

COOK

Select **SLOW COOK** and adjust to **MORE**. Cook for 5 to 6 hours or until meat is tender. Press **CANCEL**.

SERVE

Once cooking is complete, transfer ribs to a large bowl. Cover to keep warm. Skim the fat from the liquid in the pot. Select **SAUTÉ** and adjust to **NORMAL**. When liquid is simmering, add noodles and sugar snap. Return to a simmer and cook for 4 minutes. Press **CANCEL**.

Divide noodle mixture among large, flat soup bowls. Top each serving with a short rib. If desired, sprinkle with sesame seeds and spring onions.

Beef & Pork Meatloaf with Rustic Mashed Potatoes

Do your meatloaf and mashed potatoes at the same time – in the same pot – for a satisfying, home-cooked dinner.

PREP TIME	FUNCTION	CLOSED POT TIME	TOTAL TIME	RELEASE
35 minutes	Pressure/Manual (High)	60 minutes	1 hour 35 minutes + 5 minutes broil	Natural

SERVES: 8

MEATLOAF

- 2 **eggs**
- 55 **g ketchup**
- 2 **tablespoons Worcestershire sauce**
- 2 **teaspoons wholegrain mustard**
- 4 **cloves garlic, minced**
- 1 **teaspoon salt**
- 1 **teaspoon dried thyme, crushed**
- ½ **teaspoon black pepper**
- 1 **medium onion, finely chopped (about 110 g)**
- 1 **stalk celery, finely chopped**
- 60 **g dried breadcrumbs**
- 450 **minced beef**
- 450 **minced pork**

RUSTIC MASHED POTATOES

- 8 **medium Yukon gold potatoes (675 g to 900 g total), scrubbed and quartered**
- 175 **g water**
- ½ **teaspoon salt**
- 120 **ml milk**
- 2 **tablespoons butter**
   Salt and black pepper to taste

PREP

For meatloaf, in a large bowl whisk together eggs, ketchup, Worcestershire sauce, mustard, garlic, salt, thyme and pepper. Stir in onion, celery and breadcrumbs. Add beef and pork; mix well. On an 18×30-cm piece of heavy foil shape meat mixture into an 20-cm-long loaf in the centre of the foil. Wrap foil up around mixture to completely enclose the loaf. Poke several holes in the foil on the top to allow steam to escape. Set aside.

For mashed potatoes, add potatoes, water and ½ teaspoon salt to the Instant Pot®. Set wrapped meatloaf on top of potatoes in pot. Secure the lid on the pot. Close the pressure-release valve.

COOK

Select **MANUAL** and cook at high pressure for 30 minutes. When cooking is complete, use a natural release to depressurise.

SERVE

Remove the lid; carefully remove meatloaf from the pot. Unwrap meatloaf and place in a 2-litre shallow grillproof gratin dish or baking dish. Make the Sweet & Tangy Topper* and spread it evenly over the whole surface.

Grill the meatloaf 20cm from the heat for 5 to 6 minutes or until topper is heated through and just starting to bubble.

Meanwhile, drain off most of the liquid from potatoes in the pot. Add milk and butter to potatoes in pot. Use a potato masher to mash potatoes to desired texture. Season to taste with salt and pepper.

Slice meatloaf crosswise and serve with potatoes.

*SWEET & TANGY TOPPER: In a small bowl whisk together 110 g ketchup, 1 to 2 tablespoons brown sugar and 2 to 3 teaspoons spicy wholegrain mustard.

One-Pot Instant Lasagna

Love lasagna but not all of the layering – and then waiting for it to bake while hungry kids ask when dinner will be ready? The active prep time on this family-pleasing dish is just 20 minutes – quick and easy enough for any day of the week.

PREP TIME	FUNCTION	CLOSED POT TIME	TOTAL TIME	RELEASE
20 minutes	Sauté (Normal); Pressure/Manual (High)	25 minutes	45 minutes	Quick

SERVES: 8

- 225 g minced beef
- 225 g minced sausage meat
- 1 450-g box mafalda pasta or one 450-g packet lasagna sheets, broken into 4- to 5-cm pieces
- 1 900 g jar pasta sauce
- 950 ml water
- 225 g ricotta cheese
- 225 g grated mozzarella cheese

PREP
Select **SAUTÉ** on the Instant Pot® and adjust to **NORMAL**. Add minced beef and sausage meat to the pot and cook just until browned. When cooking is complete, press **CANCEL**. Stir in the pasta, pasta sauce and the water. Secure the lid on the pot. Close the pressure-release valve.

COOK
Select **MANUAL** and cook at high pressure for 5 minutes. When cooking is complete, use a quick release to depressurise.

SERVE
Stir in the ricotta cheese and half the mozzarella (mixture will look curdled from the ricotta cheese). Pour mixture into a baking tin and top with the rest of the mozzarella. If desired, place the baking tin under the grill for 2 to 3 minutes or until cheese is melted.

 Carla Bushey blogs at AdventuresofaNurse.com.

Pulled Pork with Sweet & Tangy Coleslaw

There are as many versions of this Southern-style favourite as there are cooks. This is a solid, classic take on traditional recipes that is ideal for feeding a crowd inexpensively.

PREP TIME	FUNCTION	CLOSED POT TIME	TOTAL TIME
30 minutes	Slow Cook (More)	5 hours 30 minutes	6 hours + 5 minutes stand

SERVES: 6 to 8

- 1.3 kg boneless pork shoulder, visible fat trimmed
- 25 g Barbecue Seasoning
- 60 ml water

BARBECUE SEASONING

- 55 g brown sugar
- 2 tablespoons chilli powder
- 1 tablespoon dehydrated minced onion
- 1 tablespoon garlic powder
- 1 teaspoon mustard powder
- 1 teaspoon salt
- ½ teaspoon black pepper

PREP
Cut pork into three to four portions. Make Barbecue Seasoning by combining all the ingredients in a small bowl. Sprinkle 25 g seasoning on the pork. Add the water and pork to the Instant Pot®. Secure the lid on the pot. Open the pressure-release valve.

COOK
Select **SLOW COOK** and adjust to **MORE**. Cook for 5 hours and 30 minutes.

SERVE
Remove pork to cutting board; tent with foil for 5 minutes. Shred pork using two forks and return to pot, if desired. Serve with Sweet & Tangy Coleslaw.

SWEET & TANGY COLESLAW: Combine one 450-g bag coleslaw mix, 150 g thinly sliced mini peppers, 125 g minced red onion and 2 teaspoons chopped Italian parsley in a large bowl. In a small bowl stir together 75 g mayonnaise, 2 tablespoons unseasoned rice wine vinegar, ½ teaspoon celery seed, ¼ teaspoon mustard powder, ½ teaspoon salt and ¼ teaspoon black pepper. Add to slaw; mix well and chill until ready to serve.

Mojo-Marinated Cuban-Style Pork

The bright, fresh flavours of Cuban *mojo* [MOH-hoh] – a sauce of coriander, orange, garlic, oregano and cumin – offer a way to enjoy pork shoulder apart from the more common BBQ-sauced version.

PREP TIME	FUNCTION	CLOSED POT TIME	TOTAL TIME	RELEASE
30 minutes	Meat/Stew	1 hour 5 minutes	1 hour 35 minutes + 24 hours marinate	Natural

SERVES: 8 to 10

- 60 g tightly packed fresh coriander leaves, coarsely chopped
- 1 tablespoon finely shredded orange zest
- 175 ml freshly squeezed orange juice
- 120 ml freshly squeezed lime juice
- 12 g mint leaves, coarsely chopped
- 8 cloves garlic, peeled and minced
- 2 teaspoons dried oregano
- 2 teaspoons ground cumin
- 1 teaspoon salt
- 1 teaspoon black pepper
- 120 ml extra-virgin olive oil
- 1 1.8 kg skinless, boneless pork shoulder, trimmed of excess fat

PREP

In a large non-metallic bowl combine coriander, orange zest, orange juice, lime juice, mint, garlic, oregano, cumin, salt and pepper. Mix well; reserve 120ml of the mixture for the finishing sauce; cover tightly and store in the fridge.

Add olive oil to remaining mixture in bowl. Pierce meat in several places with a small thin knife or skewer. Immerse pork shoulder in marinade, turning once to coat. Cover tightly; chill for 24 hours.

Remove pork from marinade; discard marinade. Place pork in the Instant Pot®. Secure the lid on the pot. Close the pressure-release valve.

COOK

Select **MEAT/STEW** and adjust cook time to 45 minutes. When cooking time is complete, use a natural release to depressurise.

SERVE

Transfer pork to a cutting board. Slice thinly and arrange on a serving platter. Drizzle with reserved marinade.

Pork Ragu

A *ragu* is a thick, full-bodied Italian meat sauce – usually cooked for hours on the hob to create the rich depth of flavour. This pressure-cooked version takes less time to achieve that than the traditional cooking method – and you can walk away from it.

PREP TIME	FUNCTION	CLOSED POT TIME	TOTAL TIME	RELEASE
30 minutes	Sauté (Normal); Pressure/Manual (High)	1 hour 30 minutes	2 hours	Natural

SERVES: 8

- 1.3 kg boneless pork shoulder
- 1½ teaspoons kosher salt
- ½ teaspoon black pepper
- 1 tablespoon cooking oil
- 1 medium onion, chopped
- 2 medium carrots, chopped
- 4 cloves garlic, minced
- 120 ml dry red wine
- 1 800-g tin crushed tomatoes
- 240 ml chicken stock
- 2 sprigs fresh thyme
- 1 bay leaf
- ½ teaspoon chilli flakes
- Cooked polenta or pasta

PREP
Cut pork shoulder into three equal pieces; season with salt and black pepper.

Select **SAUTÉ** on the Instant Pot® and adjust to **NORMAL**. Add oil to pot. When hot, add pork and cook for 10 minutes or until browned, turning occasionally. Remove pork to a plate. Add onion and carrots to pot; cook for 6 to 8 minutes or until browned, stirring frequently. Add garlic; cook and stir for 1 minute more. Add wine; cook and stir for 2 to 3 minutes or until most of the liquid is absorbed. Press **CANCEL**.

Stir in tomatoes, stock, thyme, bay leaf and chilli flakes. Return pork to pot. Secure the lid on the pot. Close the pressure-release valve.

COOK
Select **MANUAL** and cook at high pressure for 45 minutes. When cooking is complete, use a natural release to depressurise.

SERVE
Remove and discard thyme sprigs and bay leaf. Use two forks to shred pork in pot. Season with additional salt and black pepper.

Serve over polenta or pasta.

Any-Night Porchetta with Veggies

The classic version of this Italian dish usually calls for seasoning and stuffing the meat and then letting it marinate overnight before slow-roasting it in the oven. While this version isn't a 30-minute meal, it is certainly doable any day of the week. Better yet, it's fancy enough for a special occasion or for company on a weekend!

PREP TIME	FUNCTION	CLOSED POT TIME	TOTAL TIME	RELEASE
50 minutes	Sauté (Normal); Pressure/Manual (High)	45 minutes	1 hour 35 minutes	Quick

SERVES: 8 to 10

- 1 **1.1-kg to 1.3-kg pork loin roast**
- 1½ **teaspoons salt**
- ½ **teaspoon freshly ground black pepper**
- 4 **tablespoons olive oil**
- 4 **cloves garlic, minced**
- 1 **tablespoon chopped rosemary**
- 1 **tablespoon finely grated lemon zest**
- 1 **tablespoon fennel seeds, bruised**
- 2 **teaspoons fresh sage, chopped**
- 2 **teaspoons fresh oregano, chopped**
- 120 **ml dry white wine**
- 120 **ml chicken stock**
- 1 **large onion, coarsely chopped**
- 3 **cloves garlic, thinly sliced**
- 20 **baby potatoes, quartered**
- 2 **large carrots, coarsely chopped**
- 20 **Brussels sprouts, halved**
- 1 **teaspoon dried thyme leaves**

PREP

Butterfly the pork roast by making a lengthwise cut down the centre of the roast, cutting to within 1 cm of the other side. Spread the roast open. Place the knife in the V cut, facing it horizontally towards one side of the V and cut to within 1cm of the side. Repeat on the other side of the V. Spread the roast open and cover with cling film. Working from the centre to the edges, pound the roast until it is about 2 cm thick. Remove and discard cling film. Season with ½ teaspoon of the salt and the pepper.

In a small bowl combine 2 tablespoons of the olive oil, minced garlic, rosemary, lemon zest, fennel seeds, sage and oregano. Spread mixture evenly over meat. Roll pork loin back up; tie to secure in four places with 100%-cotton kitchen string. Cut loin crosswise in half.

Select **SAUTÉ** on the Instant Pot® and adjust to **NORMAL**. Add remaining 2 tablespoons oil to the pot. When oil is hot, roast until browned, one piece at a time, on all sides, carefully turning with tongs. Press **CANCEL**. Pour wine and chicken stock into pot. Secure the lid on the pot. Close the pressure-release valve.

COOK

Select **MANUAL** and cook at high pressure for 20 minutes. While pork cooks, combine onion, sliced garlic, potatoes, carrots, Brussels sprouts, remaining 1 teaspoon salt and thyme. Using hands, mix well.

When cooking is complete, use a quick release to depressurise. Remove meat from pot. Tent lightly with foil and let rest.

Add vegetables to pot. Secure the lid on the pot. Close the pressure-release valve. Select **MANUAL** and cook at high pressure for 3 minutes. When cooking is complete, use a quick release to depressurise.

SERVE

Remove strings from meat and cut into thin slices. Serve meat with vegetables.

Spicy Sausage-Corn Bread Stuffed Peppers

To add a slightly smoky edge to these colourful stuffed peppers, swap fire-roasted diced tomatoes for the regular ones.

PREP TIME	FUNCTION	CLOSED POT TIME	TOTAL TIME	RELEASE
30 minutes	Sauté (Normal); Pressure/Manual (High)	20 minutes	50 minutes	Quick

SERVES: 4

- 1 tablespoon cooking oil
- 1 stalk celery, thinly sliced
- 75 g chopped onion
- 3 cloves garlic, minced
- 225 g spicy chorizo sausage, chopped
- 70 g torn, trimmed fresh kale
- 200 g corn bread stuffing mix
- 170 g undrained tinned diced tomatoes
- ⅛ to ¼ teaspoon chilli flakes
- 4 medium green, red and/or yellow peppers*
- 160 ml water

PREP

Select **SAUTÉ** on the Instant Pot® and adjust to **NORMAL**. Once hot, add oil, celery and onion. Cook for 5 minutes, stirring occasionally. Stir in garlic. Transfer vegetables to a large bowl. Press **CANCEL**. Add sausage, kale, stuffing mix, tomatoes and chilli flakes to vegetables in bowl. Stir gently to combine.

Slice off the top of each pepper, reserving the tops. Use a small sharp knife to remove the seeds and membranes from the peppers, keeping the peppers intact. Spoon sausage mixture evenly into peppers, gently patting it down into the peppers.

Place trivet in the pot. Pour the water into the pot. Arrange stuffed peppers, top sides up, on the trivet. Set the pepper tops on top of the stuffed peppers. Secure the lid on the pot. Close the pressure-release valve.

COOK

Select **MANUAL** and cook at high pressure for 5 minutes. Once cooking is complete, use a quick release to depressurise.

SERVE

Carefully lift each pepper out of the pot and place on a serving platter.

*TIP: Choose peppers that have a flat, wide base.

Sausage & Mushroom Pasta Bolognese

This classic meat sauce from the northern part of Italy never goes out of style. This recipe gives you options – choose minced beef or turkey and red wine or white wine to deglaze the bottom of the pot and add flavour to the sauce.

PREP TIME	FUNCTION	CLOSED POT TIME	TOTAL TIME	RELEASE
35 minutes	Sauté (Normal); Pressure/Manual (High)	1 hour	1 hour 35 minutes	Natural

SERVES: 8

- 1 tablespoon olive oil
- 1 onion, chopped
- 2 carrots, chopped
- 2 stalks celery, chopped
- 4 cloves garlic, minced
- 450 g fresh Italian sausage, casings removed if present
- 450 g lean minced beef or turkey
- 225 g fresh cremini or button mushrooms, sliced
- 235 ml red wine or white wine
- 1 800-g tin Italian whole tomatoes, undrained and cut up
- 2 teaspoons dried oregano, crushed
- 2 teaspoons dried basil, crushed
- 1 teaspoon fennel seeds
- 20 g chopped fresh basil
  - Cooked pasta
  - Grated Parmesan cheese (optional)

PREP

Select **SAUTÉ** on the Instant Pot® and adjust to **NORMAL**. Add the olive oil to the pot. When hot, add the onion, carrots, celery and garlic. Cook for 5 minutes or until the vegetables are softened and lightly browned. Add sausage meat and minced beef or turkey. Cook, stirring occasionally, until meat is browned for about 10 minutes. Drain fat. Add mushrooms; cook for 3 more minutes.

Add wine to the pot. Simmer for 2 minutes. Press **CANCEL**. Stir in the tomatoes, oregano, basil and fennel seeds. Secure the lid on the pot. Close the pressure-release valve.

COOK

Select **MANUAL** and cook at high pressure for 15 minutes. When cooking is complete, use a natural release to depressurise.

SERVE

Stir in fresh basil. Serve sauce over cooked pasta. If desired, sprinkle each serving with Parmesan cheese.

German Pork Roast

This gorgeous one-dish meal has a decidedly German accent. Flavoured with onion, garlic, allspice and caraway and served with sauerkraut, sweet-and-sour red cabbage and apple sauce, it has the hallmarks of that country's traditional cuisine.

PREP TIME	FUNCTION	CLOSED POT TIME	TOTAL TIME	RELEASE
40 minutes	Sauté (Normal); Pressure/Manual (High, Low)	35 minutes	1 hour	Quick

SERVES: 6

- 900 g pork loin
- ½ teaspoon garlic powder
- ½ teaspoon onion powder
- ¼ teaspoon allspice
- ½ teaspoon salt
- ¼ teaspoon black pepper
- 2 tablespoons olive oil
- 6 potatoes, scrubbed and cut in half lengthwise (about 675 g)
- 6 carrots, scrubbed and trimmed (about 450 g)
- 1 red onion, sliced
- 2 cloves garlic, sliced
- 225 g sauerkraut
- 1 teaspoon caraway seeds
- Sweet-and-sour red cabbage
- Apple sauce

PREP
Pat the pork loin dry. Mix together the garlic powder, onion powder, allspice, salt and pepper. Apply the rub mixture to the pork. Set aside.

Select **SAUTÉ** on the Instant Pot® and adjust to **NORMAL**. When hot, add the oil. Season the potatoes and carrots with salt and pepper. Brown the potatoes and carrots in batches to add colour. Remove and set aside. Sauté the red onions and garlic for a few minutes and set aside with the potatoes and carrots. Add more oil to the pot, if needed and sear the pork well on all sides. Press **CANCEL**.

Place the sauerkraut and caraway seeds on top of the pork. Secure the lid on the pot. Close the pressure-release valve.

COOK
Select **MANUAL** and cook at high pressure for 12 minutes. When cooking is complete, use a quick release to depressurise. Add the potatoes, carrots, onions and garlic on top. Select **MANUAL** and cook at low pressure for 6 minutes. When cooking is complete, use a quick release to depressurise.

SERVE
Serve pork with red cabbage and apple sauce.

Jenny Hartin is the cookbook promotions manager at Eat Your Books and owner of The Cookbook Junkies.

Super-Simple BBQ Pork Spare ribs

You will be amazed at how incredibly tender these ribs get with just a few minutes of cooking time. A rib dinner doesn't have to be reserved only for the weekend!

PREP TIME	FUNCTION	CLOSED POT TIME	TOTAL TIME	RELEASE
10 minutes	Pressure/Manual (High)	50 minutes	1 hour + 10 minutes bake	Natural

SERVES: 2 to 4

- 1 onion, roughly chopped
- 2 teaspoons vanilla extract
- 240 ml apple cider or apple juice
- 1 teaspoon liquid smoke (optional)*
- 120 ml water
- 1 rack pork spare ribs
- 1½ teaspoons kosher salt or smoked salt
- 1 teaspoon black pepper
- 225 g barbecue sauce

PREP
Place the onion, vanilla, apple cider, liquid smoke, if using and the water in the Instant Pot®. Cut the rack of ribs into three to four portions so they fit in the pot. Season with salt and pepper and place in the pot. Secure the lid on the pot. Close the pressure-release valve.

COOK
Select **MANUAL** and cook at high pressure for 15 to 20 minutes.** When cooking is complete, use a natural release to depressurise.

Place ribs on a baking sheet. Pour barbecue sauce over the ribs. Cook in the oven at 200°C/400°F for 10 minutes, flipping ribs halfway through. (You can also grill the ribs or finish cooking them on a grill.)

***TIP:** If finishing in the oven, use the liquid smoke and smoked salt.

**Baby back ribs take 15 minutes and spare ribs take 20 minutes.

Jill Selkowitz blogs at ThisOldGal.com.

Braised Herb-Rubbed Pork Loin with Parsnips & Carrots

If you've never cooked parsnips, give them a try in this autumnal dish where their sweet taste pairs very nicely with pork.

PREP TIME	FUNCTION	CLOSED POT	TOTAL TIME	RELEASE
35 minutes	Sauté (Normal); Meat/Stew (Less); Steam	40 minutes	1 hour 15 minutes + 10 minutes	Natural/Quick

SERVES: 6 to 8

- 2 teaspoons dried oregano, crushed
- 1 teaspoon dried rosemary, crushed
- 1 teaspoon garlic powder
- 1 teaspoon salt
- ½ teaspoon black pepper
- ½ teaspoon dried thyme, crushed
- ½ teaspoon dried sage, crushed
- 1 1.3 kg pork loin
- 2 tablespoons olive oil
- 4 large carrots, peeled and cut into 10-cm-long sticks
- 2 large parsnips, peeled and cut into 10-cm-long sticks
- 120 ml chicken stock
- 60 ml apple cider
- 2 bay leaves
- 2 sprigs fresh rosemary

PREP

In a small bowl combine the oregano, rosemary, garlic powder, salt, pepper, thyme and sage. Rub seasoning mixture all over the pork. Select **SAUTÉ** on the Instant Pot® and adjust to **NORMAL**. Add olive oil to pot. When oil is hot, add pork. Cook pork until browned, turning once, for about 5 minutes. Remove pork from the pot. Add the carrots and parsnips. Cook, stirring occasionally, for about 10 minutes or until the vegetables are lightly browned. Press **CANCEL**. Remove vegetables from pot.

Return pork to the pot. Add the chicken stock and apple cider. Place the bay leaves and rosemary over the pork. Secure the lid on the pot. Close the pressure-release valve.

COOK

Select **MEAT/STEW** and adjust to **LESS**. When cooking is complete, use a natural release to depressurise. Return carrots and parsnips to pot. Press **CANCEL.** Secure the lid on the pot. Close the pressure-release valve. Select **STEAM** and cook for 2 minutes. When cooking is complete, use a quick release to depressurise.

SERVE

Remove pork and let rest for 10 minutes before slicing. Remove and discard bay leaves and rosemary sprigs. Use a slotted spoon to transfer carrots and parsnips to a serving dish. Serve pork with carrots, parsnips and cooking juices.

Moroccan Lamb Shanks with Dates

Pressure-cooking lamb shanks–a tough cut of meat–turns them meltingly tender and keeps them super juicy. The sauce has tremendous depth of flavour and complements the flavour of the lamb superbly.

PREP TIME	FUNCTION		CLOSED POT TIME	TOTAL TIME	RELEASE
35 minutes	Sauté (Normal); Meat/Stew (More)		1 hour 25 minutes	2 hours	Natural

SERVES: 3 to 4

- ½ teaspoon salt
- 1 tablespoon finely grated fresh ginger
- 1 tablespoon sweet paprika
- 2 teaspoons ground cumin
- 3 large lamb shanks (900 g to 1.1 kg)
- 1 tablespoon olive oil
- ½ large onion, thinly sliced
- 225 g cherry tomatoes, halved
- 120 ml apple juice
- 120 ml chicken stock
- 1 tablespoon harissa*
- 1 8-cm-long cinnamon stick
- ¼ teaspoon black pepper
- ¼ teaspoon ground coriander
- 45 g chopped dates**
- Hot cooked couscous (optional)
- 15 large Medjool dates, pitted**
- 60 g golden raisins
- 45 g slivered dried apricots
- 60 g pomegranate seeds
- 1 tablespoon coarsely chopped fresh coriander

PREP

Combine salt, ginger, paprika and cumin; mix well. Rub mixture over lamb shanks; set aside.

Select **SAUTÉ** on the Instant Pot® and adjust to **NORMAL**. Add olive oil to pot. When oil is hot, add the onion and cook and stir until starting to soften for about 3 minutes. Press **CANCEL**. Add tomatoes. Cook and stir until tomatoes start to soften for about 3 minutes. Place seasoned shanks on top of tomato-onion mixture. Add the apple juice, chicken stock, harissa, cinnamon stick, pepper, coriander and chopped dates. Secure the lid on the pot. Close the pressure-release valve.

COOK

Select **MEAT/STEW** and adjust to **MORE**. When cooking is complete, use a natural release to depressurise. Press **CANCEL**.

SERVE

If using, make a bed of couscous on a warm platter. Using a slotted spoon, transfer shanks from the pot to the platter. Select **SAUTÉ**. Add Medjool dates, raisins and apricots. Cook and stir for 3 to 4 minutes. Press **CANCEL**.

Ladle date mixture over shanks. Sprinkle with pomegranate seeds and coriander.

*TIP: Harissa is a North African condiment made of chillis, garlic, caraway, spices and olive oil. It can range from mild to fiery-hot. Choose one based on your personal taste.

**TIP: There are two types of dates called for in this recipe. Medjool dates are considered the 'king of dates'–they are large, moist, soft and creamy and have very little fibrous texture. They are added only at the end of cooking to warm through; they would completely break down if they were cooked with the lamb. The other type–more common and less expensive than the Medjool dates (often Deglet Noor dates)–are semidry and have more fibre, making them a little sturdier. They are cooked with the lamb to add flavour.

Chicken Toscana with White Beans

Setting the pressure-cook time for just 1 minute after the vegetables are added to the pot – and using a quick release to depressurise – ensures that they don't get overcooked (especially the delicate courgette!).

PREP TIME	FUNCTION	CLOSED POT TIME	TOTAL TIME	RELEASE
35 minutes	Sauté (Normal); Poultry; Pressure/Manual (High)	35 minutes	1 hour 10 minutes	Quick

SERVES: 6

- 1.3 kg bone-in chicken thighs, skin removed (about 6 thighs)
- ½ teaspoon salt
- ¼ teaspoon black pepper
- 2 tablespoons olive oil
- 1 sprig fresh rosemary
- 240 ml dry white wine
- 2 courgettes, cut into 4-cm chunks
- 225 g button mushrooms, cleaned
- 1 170-g jar marinated artichoke hearts, drained
- 170 g chopped fire-roasted red peppers, drained
- 1 170 g jar pitted Kalamata olives, drained and halved
- 350 g pappardelle or other wide noodle, cooked according to packet instructions
- 3 teaspoons finely chopped fresh flat-leaf parsley
- 2 teaspoons snipped fresh basil

PREP

Season chicken with salt and pepper. Select **SAUTÉ** on the Instant Pot® and adjust to **NORMAL**. Add the oil. When oil is hot, add rosemary sprig and stir until oil is very fragrant. Remove rosemary; discard. Working with half of the chicken at a time, brown chicken pieces on all sides in rosemary-infused oil about 5 minutes. Press **CANCEL**. Return all chicken to pot. Add wine to pot. Secure the lid on the pot. Close the pressure-release valve.

COOK

Select **POULTRY**. When cooking is complete, use a quick release to depressurise. Press **CANCEL**. Add courgettes, mushrooms, artichoke hearts, red peppers and olives.

Secure the lid on the pot. Close the pressure-release valve. Select **MANUAL** and cook at high pressure for 1 minute. When cooking is complete, use a quick release to depressurise.

SERVE

Divide cooked pappardelle among six shallow pasta bowls. Using a slotted spoon, arrange chicken pieces and vegetables over pappardelle. Ladle a small amount of juices over each serving. Sprinkle with parsley and fresh basil.

Chicken Cacciatore with Porcini Mushrooms

Cacciatore means 'hunter' in Italian. Dishes prepared 'hunter-style' refer to a common set of ingredients – usually onions, mushrooms, herbs, wine and tomatoes. The porcini mushrooms in this version of the Italian favourite add earthy, rich flavour to the dish.

PREP TIME	FUNCTION	CLOSED POT TIME	TOTAL TIME	RELEASE
35 minutes	Sauté (Normal/Less); Poultry	35 minutes	1 hour 10 minutes + 10 minutes simmer	Natural

SERVES: 4

- 1 tablespoon olive oil
- 900 g bone-in, skinned chicken thighs and/or drumsticks
- ½ teaspoon salt
- ¼ teaspoon black pepper
- 15 g dried porcini mushrooms, rinsed
- 120 ml boiling water
- 1 onion, coarsely chopped
- 1 red pepper, coarsely chopped
- 2 cloves garlic, minced
- 240 ml dry red or white wine
- 1 800-g tin whole tomatoes, undrained and coarsely cut up
- 1 teaspoon dried rosemary, crushed
- 1 teaspoon dried sage, crushed
- 1 bay leaf
- 70 g black olives, halved
- 1½ teaspoons chopped fresh flat-leaf parsley
- Cooked pasta, rice or polenta

PREP

Select **SAUTÉ** on Instant Pot® and adjust to **NORMAL**. Add oil. Season chicken with salt and pepper. When oil is hot, add chicken. Cook chicken, half at a time, until browned, turning once, for about 7 to 8 minutes.

Meanwhile, place porcini mushrooms in a small bowl and add the boiling water. Let stand for 5 minutes. Drain, reserving liquid. Chop mushrooms.

Remove chicken from pot. Add onion, red pepper and garlic. Cook, stirring occasionally, until onion is softened, for about 2 minutes. Add wine. Simmer for 2 minutes. Press **CANCEL**. Add tomatoes, rosemary, sage and the bay leaf. Stir in the mushrooms and the mushroom liquid. Return chicken to pot. Secure the lid on the pot.

COOK

Select **POULTRY**. When cooking is complete, use a natural release to depressurise. Press **CANCEL**.

SERVE

Transfer chicken to a platter; cover lightly with foil to keep warm. Skim fat from cooking liquid. Remove and discard bay leaf. Select **SAUTÉ** and adjust to **LESS**. Cook sauce for 10 minutes to reduce and slightly thicken. Press **CANCEL**.

Top chicken with sauce and vegetables, olives and parsley. Serve with pasta, rice or polenta.

Chicken Piccata

There is something irresistible about the combination of tangy lemon, briny capers, fresh herbs and the rich flavour of butter–which is perhaps why this dish retains its popularity. Serve with pasta or rice and fresh steamed green beans or sautéed spinach.

PREP TIME	FUNCTION	CLOSED POT TIME	TOTAL TIME	RELEASE
20 minutes	Sauté (Normal); Manual/Pressure (High)	10 minutes	30 minutes + 5 minutes simmer	Quick

SERVES: 4

- 4 skinless, boneless chicken breasts (675 g to 800 g)
- ½ teaspoon salt
- ¼ teaspoon black pepper
- 1 tablespoon olive oil
- 240 ml chicken stock
- 60 ml fresh lemon juice
- 2 tablespoons butter
- 2 tablespoons brined capers, drained
- 2 tablespoons chopped fresh flat-leaf parsley
- Hot cooked pasta or rice
- Lemon slices

PREP

Season the chicken with salt and pepper. Select **SAUTÉ** on the Instant Pot® and adjust to **NORMAL**. Heat oil in pot; add chicken and cook for 2 to 3 minutes per side until browned. Add stock. Press **CANCEL**. Secure the lid on the pot. Close the pressure-release valve.

COOK

Select **MANUAL** and cook at high pressure for 3 minutes. When cooking is complete, use a quick release to depressurise. Press **CANCEL**. Use tongs to remove chicken to a serving platter; cover to keep warm.

Add lemon juice to cooking liquid in pot. Select **SAUTÉ** and adjust to **NORMAL**. Bring to a simmer and cook for 5 minutes to reduce. Press **CANCEL**. Whisk butter into sauce; add capers and parsley.

SERVE

Pour sauce over chicken. Serve over pasta or rice. Serve with lemon slices.

Weeknight Chicken Marsala

Marsala is wine that has been fortified, or infused with a spirit such as brandy. It gives this dish its signature warm, smoky flavour.

PREP TIME	FUNCTION	CLOSED POT TIME	TOTAL TIME	RELEASE
30 minutes	Sauté (Normal); Poultry	30 minutes	1 hour + 8 minutes simmer	Natural

SERVES: 4

- 4 large bone-in chicken thighs (800 g to 900 g total)
- ¼ teaspoon salt
- ¼ teaspoon black pepper
- 1 to 2 tablespoons olive oil
- 225 g fresh cremini mushrooms, thickly sliced
- 2 medium shallots, thinly sliced (about 65 g)
- 2 cloves garlic, thinly sliced
- 120 ml reduced-salt chicken stock
- 80 ml sweet Marsala wine
- 80 ml whipping cream
- 1½ teaspoons chopped fresh flat-leaf parsley
- Cooked pasta (optional)

PREP

Select **SAUTÉ** on the Instant Pot® and adjust to **NORMAL**. Remove skin from chicken thighs. Sprinkle chicken with salt and pepper. Add 1 tablespoon oil to the hot pot. Add chicken thighs, bone sides up. Cook for 8 to 10 minutes or until meat is browned, flipping once halfway through cooking. Remove chicken from pot. Add mushrooms, shallots and garlic to pot. If needed, add remaining 1 tablespoon oil. Cook for 5 to 7 minutes or until mushrooms are lightly browned, stirring occasionally. Press **CANCEL**.

Add chicken stock to mushroom mixture in the pot. Lay chicken thighs on top of the mushroom mixture. Secure the lid on the pot. Close the pressure-release valve.

COOK

Select **POULTRY** and adjust cook time to 10 minutes. When cooking is complete, use a natural release to depressurise. Press **CANCEL**. Transfer chicken thighs to a serving platter. Cover to keep warm.

Select **SAUTÉ** and adjust to **NORMAL**. Add wine to mushroom mixture in pot. Bring to boiling. Boil gently for 3 minutes. Stir in whipping cream. Cook for 5 minutes more or until sauce is slightly thickened, stirring occasionally. Press **CANCEL**.

SERVE

Serve mushroom sauce over chicken. Sprinkle with parsley. If desired, serve with cooked pasta.

Chicken Burrito Bowls

Bypass the restaurants that make these fast-food favourites out of ingredients that sit for hours in a steam table. The Instant Pot® allows you to make your own fresh and fast version at home for a lot less money.

PREP TIME	FUNCTION	CLOSED POT TIME	TOTAL TIME	RELEASE
15 minutes	Pressure/Manual (High)	1 hour 5 minutes	1 hour 20 minutes	Quick

SERVES: 6

- 225 g soured cream
- 2 tablespoons chipotle sauce (from a tin of chipotle chillis in adobo)
- 2 tablespoons fresh lime juice
- 1 clove garlic, minced
- ¼ teaspoon salt
- 900 g skinless, boneless chicken breasts and/or thighs
- 1 800-g tin diced tomatoes
- 1 tablespoon smoked paprika
- 3 cloves garlic, minced
- 150 g chopped onion
- 1 teaspoon coarse salt
- ½ teaspoon black pepper
- 1 900-g pot reduced-salt chicken stock
- 1 400-g box instant whole grain brown rice
- 2 400-g tins black beans, rinsed and drained
- 230 g grated Monterey Jack or Gouda cheese
- Snipped fresh coriander

PREP

For the chipotle sauce, in a small bowl combine the soured cream, 1 tablespoon of the chipotle sauce, lime juice, 1 clove minced garlic and salt. Cover and chill until serving.

Place the chicken, diced tomatoes, the remaining 1 tablespoon chipotle sauce, paprika, 3 cloves minced garlic, onion, coarse salt, black pepper and 475 ml of the stock in the Instant Pot®. Secure the lid on the pot. Close the pressure-release valve.

COOK

Select **MANUAL** and cook at high pressure for 15 minutes. When cooking is complete, press **CANCEL** and use a quick release to depressurise. Remove the chicken from the cooking liquid.

Add the remaining stock, rice and black beans to the cooking liquid. Secure the lid on the pot. Close the pressure-release valve. Select **MANUAL** and cook at high pressure for 5 minutes. When cooking is complete, use a quick release to depressurise.

SERVE

Meanwhile, use two forks to shred the chicken. Add the chicken to the pot; stir to combine with the rice-bean mixture.

Serve in bowls topped with cheese, chipotle sauce and coriander.

Shredded Chicken Tacos

Chipotle chillis in vinegary adobo sauce add heat and smoky flavour to the filling for these quick-to-fix tacos.

PREP TIME	FUNCTION	CLOSED POT TIME	TOTAL TIME	RELEASE
25 minutes	Sauté (Normal); Pressure/Manual (High)	20 minutes	45 minutes + 5 minutes simmer	Natural

SERVES: 6

- 1 400-g tin flame-roasted diced tomatoes, undrained
- 120 ml chicken stock
- 1 to 2 tinned chipotle chillis in adobo
- 2 cloves garlic, peeled
- 1 teaspoon ground cumin
- 900 g skinless, boneless chicken thighs
- ½ teaspoon salt
- ¼ teaspoon black pepper
- 1 tablespoon olive oil
- 12 15-cm corn tortillas, warmed
- 90 g crumbled feta
- 2 tablespoons chopped fresh coriander
- Lime wedges

PREP

In a blender combine tomatoes, stock, chipotle, garlic and cumin. Cover and blend until smooth.

Season the chicken with salt and pepper. Select **SAUTÉ** on the Instant Pot® and adjust to **NORMAL**. Heat oil in pot; add chicken and cook for 2 to 3 minutes per side until browned. Add the blended tomato mixture. Press **CANCEL**. Secure the lid on the pot. Close the pressure-release valve.

COOK

Select **MANUAL** and cook at high pressure for 5 minutes. When cooking is complete, use a natural release to depressurise. Press **CANCEL**. Use tongs to remove chicken to a cutting board; shred chicken with a fork.

For a thicker sauce, select **SAUTÉ** and adjust to **NORMAL**. Bring sauce to a simmer. Cook for 5 minutes to reduce, stirring frequently. Add shredded chicken to pot; heat through. Press **CANCEL**.

SERVE

Serve chicken mixture in tortillas topped with feta and coriander. Serve with lime wedges.

Chicken Tamales

Steaming neat little packages of flavourful chicken filling surrounded by a rich masa dough is a perfect job for the Instant Pot®. Each bite is savoury, toothsome and absolutely delicious!

PREP TIME	FUNCTION	CLOSED POT TIME	TOTAL TIME	RELEASE
1 hour	Pressure/Manual (High)	35 minutes	2 hours 30 minutes + 1 hour soak	Quick

SERVES: 4 to 6

20	dried corn husks
510	g masa harina (maize meal)
480	ml chicken stock
225	g shortening or lard
1½	teaspoons salt
1	teaspoon baking powder
310	g shredded cooked chicken
200	g salsa verde tomatillo salsa
12	g chopped fresh coriander
1	serrano pepper, seeded and chopped
2	cloves garlic, minced
480	ml water
	Tamale sauce

PREP

Place corn husks in a large bowl. Cover with warm water and soak until soft and pliable for at least 1 hour.

For dough, in a medium bowl combine masa harina and stock. In a large bowl beat shortening, salt and baking powder with an electric mixer until light and fluffy for about 1 minute. Add half of the masa mixture and beat until well blended. Add remaining masa mixture and beat until a soft dough forms. If needed, beat in additional stock, adding 1 tablespoon at a time.

For filling, in a medium bowl combine chicken, salsa, coriander, serrano and garlic.

Drain the corn husks and pat dry. Spread 3 to 4 tablespoons dough down centre of a husk, leaving a 2.5-cm border on the sides. Spoon about 2 tablespoons chicken filling over dough. Fold sides of the husk, wrapping the dough around the filling and pressing gently to close. Fold the husk closed on both sides to make a neat package. Repeat with remaining husks, dough and filling.

Place a vegetable steamer basket in the Instant Pot®. Add the water to pot and place tamales in steamer basket. Secure the lid on the pot. Close the pressure-release valve.

COOK

Select **MANUAL** and cook at high pressure for 25 minutes. When cooking is complete, use a quick release to depressurise.

SERVE

Serve with tamale sauce.

Easy Chicken Bouillabaisse

Traditional bouillabaisse is a French tomato-based seafood stew. Here, the same treatment is given to chicken. The toasted garlic bread is for sopping up the delicious stock flavoured with fennel, thyme, white wine, orange juice and garlic.

PREP TIME	FUNCTION	CLOSED POT TIME	TOTAL TIME	RELEASE
35 minutes	Sauté (More/Normal); Meat/Stew	50 minutes	1 hour 15 minutes	Natural

SERVES: 6

- 2 tablespoons olive oil
- 6 skinless, boneless chicken thighs (675 g)
- 2 medium fennel bulbs, cut into wedges (reserve 2 tablespoons fronds)
- 1 large onion, halved and thinly sliced
- 2 bay leaves
- 1 large sprig fresh thyme
- ¼ teaspoon chilli flakes
- 480 ml chicken stock
- 1 400-g tin flame-roasted diced tomatoes
- 240 ml dry white wine
- 80 ml orange juice
- 2 cloves garlic, minced
- 1 tablespoon finely grated orange zest

  Toasted garlic bread

PREP

Select **SAUTÉ** on the Instant Pot® and adjust to **MORE**. Add oil to pot. Cook chicken, half at a time, until golden brown, for about 10 minutes. Transfer chicken to a clean plate; set aside. Press **CANCEL**. Select **SAUTÉ** and adjust to **NORMAL**. Add fennel and onion to pot. Cook and stir until slightly softened for about 10 minutes. Return chicken to pot. Add bay leaves, thyme, chilli flakes, chicken stock, tomatoes, wine, orange juice and garlic. Press **CANCEL**. Secure lid on pot. Close the pressure-release valve.

COOK

Select **MEAT/STEW** and adjust cook time to 8 minutes. When cooking is complete, use a natural release to depressurise.

SERVE

Place 1 chicken thigh in each of six soup bowls. Remove and discard bay leaves. Ladle fennel, onion and juices over the tops. Combine snipped reserved fennel fronds with orange zest and sprinkle over chicken.

Serve with toasted garlic bread.

Italian Summer Supper Salad with Chicken

Originally devised as a way to use up day-old bread, this bread and tomato salad–called *panzanella* in Italy–is best made with ripe, juicy summer tomatoes. It doesn't usually contain chicken, but adding it turns a side dish into a meal.

PREP TIME	FUNCTION		CLOSED POT TIME	TOTAL TIME	RELEASE
15 minutes	Poultry		1 hour 15 minutes	1 hour 30 minutes	Natural

SERVES: 6

- 1 whole 1.1-kg to 1.3-kg chicken, skinned
- 60 ml olive oil
- ½ teaspoon dried thyme
- ½ teaspoon dried sage
- 240 ml water
- 200 g 2.5-cm cubes of Italian country bread, toasted*
- 3 medium heirloom tomatoes, cut into wedges
- 1 cucumber, halved and cut into 1-cm-thick slices
- ½ red onion, peeled, halved and thinly sliced
- 60 ml red wine vinegar
- 1 clove garlic, minced
- 80 ml extra virgin olive oil
- ½ teaspoon coarse salt
- Black pepper
- 20 large basil leaves, torn
- Parmesan shavings (optional)

PREP

Rub outside of chicken with the 60 ml oil; sprinkle with thyme and sage. Place the trivet in the pot. Pour the water into the Instant Pot®. Place chicken on trivet. Secure the lid on the pot. Close the pressure-release valve.

COOK

Select **POULTRY** and adjust to 45 minutes cooking time. When cooking is complete, use a natural release to depressurise. Remove chicken from pot and allow to cool slightly.

SERVE

While chicken cooks, in a large salad bowl combine toasted breadcubes, tomatoes, cucumber and red onion. In a jar with a tight-fitting lid combine vinegar, garlic and the 80 ml olive oil.

When chicken is warm but not hot, use two forks to pull meat from bones into large bite-size pieces. Add chicken to bowl; toss gently. Shake dressing vigorously and drizzle over all ingredients in bowl. Season salad with the salt and pepper to taste. Toss gently.

Sprinkle basil over top of salad. If desired, top with Parmesan shavings. Enjoy salad warm or at room temperature.

*TIP: To toast the bread, toss the cubes with 2 tablespoons olive oil and spread in a single layer on a rimmed baking sheet. Toast in a 140°C/275°F oven for about 20 minutes or until very lightly browned. Let cool completely before using.

Peruvian Chicken Bowls with Green Sauce

This dish is suited to lovers of fiery food! The creamy avocado sauce cools it down a bit, but if you would prefer it less spicy, cut the amount of yellow pepper paste to 2 tablespoons.

PREP TIME	FUNCTION	CLOSED POT TIME	TOTAL TIME	RELEASE
35 minutes	Pressure/Manual (High)	40 minutes	1 hour 15 minutes	Quick

SERVES: 4

CHICKEN

- 60 ml aji amarillo (yellow hot pepper) paste*
- 1 tablespoon white vinegar
- 1 tablespoon olive oil
- 675 g skinless, boneless chicken thighs, diced into 4-cm pieces
- 180 ml reduced-salt chicken stock
- 450 g small red potatoes (4 cm to 5 cm in diameter), quartered
- 175 g fresh or frozen corn kernels

SAUCE

- pulp of 1 medium avocado
- Juice of 1 lime
- 50 g fresh coriander leaves
- 1 jalapeño pepper, coarsely chopped (seeds removed, optional)
- 60 ml white vinegar
- 30 g crumbled feta cheese
- 60 ml water
- ¼ teaspoon salt
- coriander
- cheese

PREP

Combine pepper paste, vinegar and oil in a bowl. Add chicken and toss to coat.

Pour 120 ml of the stock into the Instant Pot®. Layer in the chicken, potatoes and corn. Pour remaining 60 ml stock over all. Secure the lid on the pot. Close the pressure-release valve.

COOK

Select **MANUAL** and cook at high pressure for 10 minutes. When cooking is complete, use a quick release to depressurise.

While chicken is cooking, make the sauce: Process avocado, lime juice, coriander, jalapeño, vinegar, cheese and the water in a food processor or blender until smooth. Taste and season with desired amount of salt. Chill until ready to use.

SERVE

Divide chicken, potatoes and corn among bowls. Drizzle with green sauce. If desired, sprinkle with additional coriander and cheese.

*TIP: Aji amarillo and aji mirasol are both types of Peruvian hot peppers. If you can't find the jarred paste in the Mexican section of your supermarket, try a Hispanic market. They are also both available online.

Moroccan Chicken Tagine

This savoury North African stew is named for its traditional cooking pot – the tagine – which is an earthenware utensil with a concave conical lid. Its unusual lid shape allows aromatic steam to condense and flow back into the food, adding flavour. The Instant Pot® performs the same vital task.

PREP TIME	FUNCTION	CLOSED POT TIME	TOTAL TIME	RELEASE
30 minutes	Sauté (Normal); Meat/Stew (Less)	1 hour	1 hour 30 minutes	Natural

SERVES: 6 to 8

- 2 teaspoons ground turmeric
- 2 teaspoons ground cumin
- 1 teaspoon ground coriander
- 1 teaspoon salt
- ½ teaspoon black pepper
- 8 skinless, boneless chicken thighs
- 2 tablespoons olive oil
- 1 medium red onion, peeled and thinly sliced
- 3 cloves garlic, minced
- 300 g dried brown lentils
- 85 g chopped, pitted Medjool dates
- 85 g halved pitted green olives
- 2 cinnamon sticks
- 60 ml dry white wine
- 480 ml chicken stock
- 1 bunch fresh coriander, tied together with kitchen string
- Snipped coriander
- Lemon wedges

PREP

In a small bowl combine the turmeric, cumin, coriander, salt and pepper. Mix well. Sprinkle chicken thighs evenly with spice mixture.

Add oil to the Instant Pot®. Select **SAUTÉ** and adjust to **NORMAL**. Working two at a time, brown thighs on both sides. Transfer thighs to a plate; set aside.

Add onion to the oil remaining in the pot; cook and stir for 2 minutes. Add garlic; cook and stir for 1 minute more. Add lentils, dates, olives, cinnamon sticks, wine and chicken stock. Place coriander bundle on top of chicken. Press **CANCEL**.

Secure the lid on the pot. Close the pressure-release valve.

COOK

Select **MEAT/STEW** and adjust cook time to **LESS**. When cooking is complete, use a natural release to depressurise.

SERVE

Remove coriander bundle and discard.

Transfer cooked chicken to a plate. Spoon lentil mixture into a shallow bowl or onto plates; arrange thighs on top of lentils. Sprinkle with coriander and serve with lemon wedges.

Thai Green Curry Chicken

Craving curry? Skip the take-away and make it yourself in just a little more than 30 minutes.

PREP TIME	FUNCTION	CLOSED POT TIME	TOTAL TIME	RELEASE
15 minutes	Sauté (Normal); Pressure/Manual (High)	20 minutes	35 minutes	Quick

SERVES: 4

- 1 tablespoon coconut oil
- 1 shallot, thinly sliced
- 1 tablespoon minced fresh ginger
- 1 serrano pepper, seeded and minced
- 450 g skinless, boneless chicken breast, thinly sliced*
- ½ teaspoon salt
- 1 400-g tin coconut milk, shaken
- 55 g Thai green chilli paste
- 2 carrots, thinly sliced
- 225 g green beans, trimmed
- 1 medium yellow or red sweet pepper, cut into strips
- Hot cooked jasmine rice
- 4 lime wedges
- 2 teaspoons chopped fresh coriander leaves
- 2 teaspoons thinly sliced fresh basil leaves
- 35 g coarsely chopped roasted and salted cashews

PREP

Select **SAUTÉ** on the Instant Pot® and adjust to **NORMAL**. Add oil to pot. When oil is hot, add shallot, ginger and pepper. Cook and stir until aromatics are slightly wilted for about 2 minutes. Add chicken to pot. Season with salt. Cook and stir just until no longer pink for about 3 minutes. Press **CANCEL**.

Add coconut milk and chilli paste to pot. Stir until combined. Stir in carrots, green beans and sweet pepper. Secure the lid on the pot. Close the pressure-release valve.

COOK

Select **MANUAL** and cook at high pressure for 4 minutes. When cooking is complete, use a quick release to depressurise.

SERVE

Serve over hot cooked jasmine rice with lime wedges for squeezing. Top with coriander, basil and cashews.

*TIP: Place chicken breast in freezer for 30 minutes prior to slicing to cut thin, evenly sized pieces.

General Tso's Chicken

This intensely flavoured sweet-and-spicy dish tastes just like the one with the same name from your favourite Chinese restaurant.

PREP TIME	FUNCTION	CLOSED POT TIME	TOTAL TIME	RELEASE
25 minutes	Sauté (Normal); Pressure/Manual (High)	20 minutes	45 minutes	Quick

SERVES: 6

- 1 teaspoon sesame oil
- 675 g skinless, boneless chicken breast and/or thighs, cubed
- 6 tablespoons rice vinegar
- 6 tablespoons soy sauce
- 1 clove garlic, chopped
- ¼ teaspoon ground ginger
- ¼ teaspoon chilli flakes
- 170 g hoisin sauce
- 4 tablespoons brown sugar
- 2 tablespoons cornflour
- 500 g cooked white rice
- 1 spring onion, chopped
- Sesame seeds

PREP

Pour the sesame oil in the Instant Pot®. Select **SAUTÉ** and adjust to **NORMAL**. Add chicken to the pot. Cook and stir for 5 minutes or until chicken is white (does not need to be cooked all the way through). Press **CANCEL**.

In a separate bowl mix together the rice vinegar, soy sauce, garlic, ginger, chilli flakes, hoisin sauce and brown sugar. Pour the mixture over the chicken in the pot. Secure the lid on the pot. Close the pressure-release valve.

COOK

Select **MANUAL** and cook at high pressure for 10 minutes. When cooking is complete, use a quick release to depressurise. Press **CANCEL**.

Select **SAUTÉ** and adjust to **NORMAL**. Bring to a slight boil. Whisk in the cornflour until mixture turns thick and bubbly for about 2 minutes. Press **CANCEL**.

SERVE

Serve the chicken over rice. Sprinkle with spring onions and sesame seeds.

 Carla Bushey blogs at AdventuresofaNurse.com.

Spanish Arroz con Pollo

This creamy one-pot rice-and-chicken dish gets its pungent flavour, aroma and sunny yellow colour from saffron – the stems of a type of crocus flower. It's a very pricey spice, so if you want to skip it, you can – but it won't be quite the same.

PREP TIME	FUNCTION	CLOSED POT TIME	TOTAL TIME	RELEASE
35 minutes	Sauté (Normal); Pressure/Manual (High)	55 minutes	1 hour 30 minutes + 5 minutes	Natural

SERVES: 4 to 6

- ½ teaspoon saffron threads, crushed (optional)
- 3 tablespoons warm water (optional)
- 1.1 kg chicken breasts, thighs and/ or drumsticks (bone-in, skin removed)
- ½ teaspoon salt
- ¼ teaspoon black pepper
- 2 tablespoons olive oil
- 150 g chopped onion
- 1 medium red pepper, sliced
- 3 cloves garlic, minced
- 1 400-g tin diced tomatoes, undrained
- 1½ teaspoons paprika
- 1½ teaspoons dried oregano, crushed
- ⅛ teaspoon chilli flakes
- 150 ml dry white wine or chicken stock
- 360 ml water or chicken stock
- 225 g short grain white rice
- 75 g fresh or frozen peas
- 85 g pimiento-stuffed green olives, sliced

PREP

If using, in a small bowl combine the saffron and the warm water. Set aside.

Season the chicken with the salt and black pepper. Select **SAUTÉ** on the Instant Pot and adjust to **NORMAL**. Add oil to pot. When the oil is hot, working with half the chicken at a time, brown chicken pieces on all sides. Remove the chicken to a plate. Add the onion, pepper and garlic to the pot. Cook for 3 to 5 minutes or until crisp-tender. Press **CANCEL**. Add the chicken, tomatoes, paprika, oregano, chilli flakes, wine, the 360 ml water, rice and, if using, saffron. Secure the lid on the pot. Close the pressure-release valve.

COOK

Select **MANUAL** and cook at high pressure for 15 minutes. When cooking is complete, use a natural release to depressurise.

SERVE

Fluff the rice with a fork. Add the peas to the pot and let stand for 5 minutes to warm through. Sprinkle servings with the sliced olives.

Cheesy Chicken Instant Mac with Veggies

Make this from-scratch mac and cheese in your Instant Pot® and you will never make it any other way again! The whole family will gobble it up – veggies and all.

PREP TIME	FUNCTION	CLOSED POT TIME	TOTAL TIME	RELEASE
25 minutes	Pressure/Manual (High); Sauté (Less)	35 minutes	1 hour	Quick

SERVES: 6

- **350 g** skinless, boneless chicken breast halves (2 small)
- **½ teaspoon** salt
- **¼ teaspoon** black pepper
- **120 ml** water
- **225 g** dried macaroni
- **2** carrots, thinly sliced
- **1** small onion, chopped
- **3** cloves garlic, minced
- **1 tablespoon** butter
- **710 ml** water
- **230 g** grated cheddar cheese
- **115 g** cream cheese, cut into cubes
- **180 ml** single cream
- **100 g** coarsely torn fresh spinach (optional)

PREP

Sprinkle chicken with ¼ teaspoon of the salt and the pepper. Place the trivet in the bottom of the Instant Pot®. Add the 120 ml water to the pot. Place chicken on trivet in a single layer. Secure the lid on the pot. Close the pressure-release valve.

COOK

Select **MANUAL** and cook at high pressure for 7 minutes. When cooking is complete, use a quick release to depressurize. Transfer chicken to a cutting board; set aside. Remove trivet from pot. Discard liquid. Add macaroni, carrots, onion, garlic, butter and remaining ¼ teaspoon salt to pot. Pour the 710 ml water over all in pot. Secure the lid on the pot. Close the pressure-release valve.

Select **MANUAL** and cook at high pressure for 2 minutes. When cooking is complete, use a natural release to depressurise. Press **CANCEL**. Do not drain off liquid.

Add cheddar cheese, cream cheese and single cream to macaroni mixture in pot. Select **SAUTÉ** and adjust to **LESS.** Cook and stir for 2 to 3 minutes or until cheese is melted and mixture is well combined. Press **CANCEL**.

SERVE

Chop the chicken. Stir into hot macaroni and cheese. If desired, stir in spinach just before serving.

HAM & PEAS CHEESY CHICKEN INSTANT MAC WITH VEGGIES: Prepare as directed except add 1 to 2 tablespoons Dijon mustard with the cream. Stir in 110 g chopped cooked ham and 110 g frozen (thawed) shelled green peas with the chicken. Continue to cook for 2 minutes to heat through, stirring frequently.

CHEESY CHICKEN INSTANT MAC WITH SALSA: Prepare as directed except stir in 170g jarred salsa with the chicken at the end.

Indian Butter Chicken

This dish of juicy chicken thighs served in a slightly spicy, luxuriously rich tomato cream sauce will be a hit with even the least adventurous eaters in your family.

PREP TIME	FUNCTION	CLOSED POT TIME	TOTAL TIME	RELEASE
35 minutes	Sauté (Normal); Poultry	45 minutes	1 hour 20 minutes	Natural

SERVES: 4

- 8   skinless, boneless chicken thighs
- 2   tablespoons garam masala
- 1   teaspoon salt
- 1   teaspoon black pepper
- 4   tablespoons butter
- 1   onion, chopped
- 1   jalapeño pepper, seeded and finely chopped
- 4   cloves garlic, minced
- 1   tablespoon minced fresh ginger
- 1   teaspoon ground cumin
- ½   teaspoon ground turmeric
- 1   400-g tin diced tomatoes
- 1   225-g tin tomato sauce
- 120   ml chicken stock
- 120   ml double cream
- 25   g chopped fresh coriander
- Cooked white rice

PREP
Sprinkle the chicken thighs with 1 tablespoon of the garam masala, the salt and black pepper; rub into chicken with fingers. Select **SAUTÉ** on the Instant Pot® and adjust to **NORMAL**. Add 2 tablespoons of the butter. When the butter is melted, add half the chicken. Cook chicken until browned, turning once, for about 10 minutes. Remove chicken from pot. Repeat with remaining chicken.

Add onion and the remaining 2 tablespoons butter. Cook, stirring occasionally, until onions are lightly browned, for about 5 minutes. Add the jalapeño, garlic and ginger. Cook and stir for 2 minutes more. Add the remaining 1 tablespoon garam masala, the cumin and turmeric. Cook and stir for 1 minute. Press **CANCEL**. Stir in the diced tomatoes, tomato sauce and chicken stock. Place the chicken on sauce. Secure the lid on the pot. Close the pressure-release valve.

COOK
Select **POULTRY**. When cooking is complete, use a natural release to depressurise.

SERVE
Stir in cream and coriander. Serve over cooked white rice.

Chicken, Broccoli & Carrots
with Curry Peanut Sauce

The sauce in this Thai-inspired one-pot dish has a little kick, but it's still very family-friendly – perfect for those busy weeknights!

PREP TIME	FUNCTION	CLOSED POT TIME	TOTAL TIME
35 minutes	Sauté (Normal); Slow Cook (More)	2 hours 25 minutes	2 hours 30 minutes

SERVES: 6

- 1 tablespoon olive oil
- 50 g chopped spring onions (half bunch)
- 4 cloves garlic, minced
- 1 5-cm piece fresh ginger, peeled and minced
- 900 g to 1.1 kg skinless, boneless chicken thighs, cut into 4-cm pieces
- 1 teaspoon kosher salt
- 475 ml low-salt chicken stock
- 125 g smooth peanut butter
- 2 tablespoons soy sauce
- 1 tablespoon fish sauce
- 2 tablespoons red curry paste
- 525 g broccoli florets
- 150 g carrots, sliced on the diagonal
- 1 tablespoon cornflour
- 2 tablespoons cold water
- Hot cooked rice
- Chopped fresh coriander
- 25 g chopped spring onions
- Chopped roasted peanuts (optional)
- Sriracha sauce

PREP

Select **SAUTÉ** on the Instant Pot® and adjust to **NORMAL**. Add the oil. When hot, add the spring onions, garlic and ginger; cook for 1 minute. Press **CANCEL**. Add the chicken to the pot and sprinkle with salt. Add the stock, peanut butter, soy sauce, fish sauce and curry paste; stir to combine. Secure the lid on the pot. Open the pressure-release valve.

COOK

Select **SLOW COOK** and adjust to **MORE**. Cook for 2 hours or until chicken is cooked through. Stir in the broccoli and carrots. Cook, covered, for 25 to 30 minutes or until the vegetables are crisp-tender. Press **CANCEL**.

Combine cornflour and the cold water in a small bowl. Stir into pot. Select **SAUTÉ** and adjust to **NORMAL**. Cook and stir for 2 to 3 minutes or until sauce is slightly thickened. Press **CANCEL**.

SERVE

Serve the chicken, vegetables and sauce over hot cooked rice. Top with coriander, onions and, if desired, peanuts. Pass the sriracha.

Light Chicken Stroganoff

Love the rich flavour of beef stroganoff but trying to lighten things up? Try this version made with chicken thighs in a yogurt-based sauce served over wholegrain noodles.

PREP TIME	FUNCTION		CLOSED POT TIME	TOTAL TIME	RELEASE
30 minutes	Sauté (Normal); Manual/Pressure (High)		15 minutes	45 minutes	Quick

SERVES: 6

- 1 350-g packet wholegrain wide noodles
- 2 tablespoons olive oil
- 2 skinless, boneless chicken breasts, cut into bite-size pieces
- 4 skinless, boneless chicken thighs, cut into bite-size pieces
- 3 large leeks, cleaned and thinly sliced (white parts only)
- 450 g button mushrooms, stems and caps thickly sliced
- 2 teaspoons fresh thyme leaves
- 120 ml dry white wine
- 1 tablespoon Worcestershire sauce
- ½ teaspoon salt
- ¼ teaspoon black pepper
- 2 teaspoons Dijon mustard
- 450 g plain low-fat yogurt
- 2 tablespoons plain flour
- 1 teaspoon paprika
- 1½ teaspoons chopped fresh flat-leaf parsley

PREP
In a large pot of boiling salted water cook noodles according to packet instructions.

While noodles cook, select **SAUTÉ** on the Instant Pot® and adjust to **NORMAL**. Add olive oil to pot. Brown chicken pieces in oil for about 10 minutes. Add leeks and mushrooms; continue to cook and stir for 2 to 3 minutes or until leeks soften.

Stir in thyme, wine, Worcestershire sauce, salt and pepper. Press **CANCEL**. Secure the lid on the pot. Close the pressure-release valve.

COOK
Select **MANUAL** and cook at high pressure for 5 minutes. When cooking is complete, use a quick release to depressurise. Press **CANCEL**. In a small bowl stir together mustard, yogurt and flour. Add to pot. Press **SAUTÉ** and adjust to **NORMAL**. Cook and stir for 2 minutes or until slightly thickened. Press **CANCEL**.

SERVE
Spoon stroganoff over noodles. Sprinkle lightly with paprika and chopped parsley.

Teriyaki Turkey

Sure, you can use the bottled stuff, but it's so easy to stir up a homemade teriyaki sauce and the flavour is so much better and fresher.

PREP TIME	FUNCTION	CLOSED POT TIME	TOTAL TIME	RELEASE
15 minutes	Sauté (Normal); Poultry	30 minutes	45 minutes	Natural

SERVES: 4

- 1 tablespoon vegetable oil
- 450 g to 675 g turkey breast fillets (about 2 breast fillets)
- 180 ml ponzu or soy sauce
- 60 ml mirin or white wine
- 55 g brown sugar
- 1 tablespoon minced fresh ginger
- 3 cloves garlic, minced
- ¼ teaspoon ground white pepper
- Dash cayenne pepper
- 1 tablespoon cornflour mixed with 2 tablespoons cold water

PREP

Select **SAUTÉ** on the Instant Pot® and adjust to **NORMAL**. When hot, add the oil to the pot. Add the turkey and cook for 8 to 10 minutes or until evenly browned. Press **CANCEL**. Drain fat.

Combine ponzu, mirin, brown sugar, ginger, garlic, white pepper and cayenne pepper in a bowl. Mix well. Pour over the turkey. Secure the lid on the pot. Close the pressure-release valve.

COOK

Select **POULTRY** and adjust cook time to 8 minutes. When cooking is complete, use a natural release to depressurise. Press **CANCEL**. Remove turkey to a serving plate. Let rest for 5 minutes, then slice.

Select **SAUTÉ** on the pot and adjust to **NORMAL**. When the cooking juices come to a boil, whisk in the cornflour mixture and cook for 1 minute. Press **CANCEL**.

SERVE

Pour sauce over the turkey or serve on the side.

Turkey Tikka Masala

Chicken tikka masala is often the first Indian dish many people try – and then they're hooked. This version swaps turkey breast for the chicken, but the other flavour elements are all there – particularly the gingery tomato-coconut milk sauce. Serve it over aromatic, nutty-flavoured basmati rice.

PREP TIME	FUNCTION	CLOSED POT TIME	TOTAL TIME	RELEASE
15 minutes	Sauté (Normal); Pressure/Manual (High)	25 minutes	40 minutes + 4 hours marinating	Quick

SERVES: 6

170 g plain yogurt

1 tablespoon freshly squeezed lemon juice

2 teaspoons black pepper

1 tablespoon cumin

1 teaspoon chilli flakes

1 teaspoon ground cinnamon

1 teaspoon salt

1 5-cm piece fresh ginger, peeled and grated

2 turkey breast fillets (675 g), patted dry

2 tablespoons vegetable oil

1 medium onion, coarsely chopped

3 cloves garlic, minced

1 400-g tin flame-roasted diced tomatoes, undrained

120 ml coconut milk

Hot cooked basmati rice

1½ teaspoons chopped fresh basil leaves

1 tablespoon chopped fresh coriander

PREP
Combine yogurt, lemon juice, black pepper, cumin, chilli flakes, cinnamon, salt and half of the ginger in a 4.5-litre resealable plastic bag. Massage to combine. Add turkey; press to immerse in marinade. Seal bag tightly. Chill for at least 4 hours or overnight.

Select **SAUTÉ** on the Instant Pot® and adjust to **NORMAL**. Add oil to pot. When hot, add onion, garlic and remaining ginger. Cook, stirring constantly, for 3 to 4 minutes or until paste forms. Press **CANCEL**. Stir in tomatoes and turkey. Secure the lid on the pot. Close the pressure-release valve.

COOK
Select **MANUAL** and cook at high pressure for 8 minutes. Once cooking is complete, use a quick release to depressurise.

SERVE
Remove turkey from pot and transfer to a cutting board. Using two forks, pull breasts into bite-size pieces. Return turkey to pot. Add coconut milk. Stir to combine. Serve over basmati rice. Sprinkle with basil and coriander.

Bacon-Cheddar Turkey Meatloaf with Caramelised Onions

Serve this yummy meatloaf with mashed potatoes and steamed green beans.

PREP TIME	FUNCTION	CLOSED POT TIME	TOTAL TIME	RELEASE
30 minutes	Sauté (Normal); Meat/Stew	1 hour 10 minutes	1 hour 40 minutes + 5 minutes stand	Natural

SERVES: 6

- 225 g sliced bacon, chopped
- 1 medium onion, chopped
- 240 ml water
- 1 egg
- 2 tablespoons barbecue sauce
- 1 tablespoon chili powder
- 2 cloves garlic, minced
- ¼ teaspoon black pepper
- 115 g grated cheddar cheese
- 50 g instant oats
- 450 g to 675 g minced turkey
- 55 g barbecue sauce
- Soured cream (optional)
- Fresh chives, snipped (optional)

PREP

Select **SAUTÉ** on the Instant Pot® and adjust to **NORMAL**. When hot, add bacon and onion. Cook until bacon is crisp and onion is tender and browned, stirring occasionally, for 4 to 5 minutes. Press **CANCEL**. Transfer bacon and onion to a small bowl using a slotted spoon. Carefully pour bacon grease from pot and discard. Place trivet in pot. Add the water to pot.

For meatloaf, in a large bowl whisk together egg, the 2 tablespoons barbecue sauce, chili powder, garlic and pepper. Stir in half the cheese and all the oats. Add turkey and the bacon mixture; mix well. On a 12×20-cm piece of heavy foil shape meat mixture into an 20-cm-long loaf in the centre of the foil. Holding the ends of the foil, lower the meatloaf down into the pot until it rests on the trivet. Tuck foil into pot as needed to allow the lid to go on. Secure the lid on the pot. Close the pressure-release valve.

COOK

Select **MEAT/STEW**. When cooking is complete, use a natural release to depressurise.

SERVE

Carefully remove meatloaf from the pot by lifting the ends of foil. Transfer meatloaf to a platter. Spoon the 55 g barbecue sauce over the top of the meatloaf. Sprinkle with remaining cheese. Let stand for 5 minutes before serving. If desired, serve with soured cream sprinkled with chives.

Fish & Shellfish

Lemony Steamed Salmon with Dill-Caper Mayonnaise

Serve this Scandinavian-style salmon warm or chill it in the fridge for a few hours and serve it cold.

PREP TIME	FUNCTION	CLOSED POT TIME	TOTAL TIME	RELEASE
20 minutes	Pressure/Manual (High)	10 minutes	30 minutes	Quick

SERVES: 4

DILL-CAPER MAYONNAISE

- 110 g olive-oil mayonnaise
- 110 g plain Greek yogurt
- 2 tablespoons minced red onion
- 2 tablespoons capers, rinsed and drained
- 1 tablespoon freshly squeezed lemon juice
- 1 tablespoon finely chopped fresh dill

SALMON

- Juice of 2 large lemons (120 ml)
- 240 ml dry white wine
- 2 cloves garlic, smashed
- 3 sprigs of parsley
- 4 115-g fresh salmon fillets, about 2 cm thick
- 2 teaspoons finely grated lemon zest

PREP

For Dill-Caper Mayonnaise, combine mayonnaise, yogurt, red onion, capers, 1 tablespoon lemon juice and the dill in a small bowl. Mix well. Cover. Sauce may be made 1 day ahead and chilled.

For the fish, combine lemon juice (and juiced lemon shells), wine, garlic and parsley in the Instant Pot®. Place trivet in pot. Fold thin sides of salmon fillets under thick sides; arrange folded fillets on trivet. Sprinkle fillets with lemon zest. Secure the lid on the pot. Close the pressure-release valve.

COOK

Select **MANUAL** and cook at high pressure for 2 minutes. When cooking is complete, use a quick release to depressurise.

SERVE

Serve salmon with Dill-Caper Mayonnaise.

Salmon with Miso Butter

Miso gives the butter a savoury, pleasantly salty, umami flavour. You can use any type of miso. From mildest to most pungent, they are white, yellow and red.

PREP TIME	FUNCTION	CLOSED POT TIME	TOTAL TIME	RELEASE
35 minutes	Manual (Pressure/Low)	10 minutes	45 minutes	Quick

SERVES: 4

- 240 ml water
- 1 lemon, halved
- 4 115-g to 150-g salmon fillets
- ¼ teaspoon salt
- ⅛ teaspoon black pepper
- 55 g butter, softened
- 4 teaspoons miso paste
- ⅛ teaspoon chilli flakes
- 1 tablespoon chopped fresh chives
- Romaine Slaw

PREP
Place trivet in Instant Pot®. Add the water to pot. Squeeze one half of the lemon into the water. Place salmon fillets in steamer basket; squeeze other half of lemon over the fish. Sprinkle with salt and black pepper. Secure the lid on the pot. Close the pressure-release valve.

COOK
Select **MANUAL** and cook at low pressure for 2 minutes. When cooking is complete, use a quick release to depressurise.

SERVE
Meanwhile, for miso butter, in a small bowl combine butter, miso and chilli flakes; mix well. Stir in chives.

Serve salmon with miso butter and the Romaine Slaw.

ROMAINE SLAW: In a large bowl combine 2 small romaine hearts, shredded; 4 radishes, halved and thinly sliced; 2 cucumbers, halved and thinly sliced; 2 spring onions, sliced; and 1 tablespoon chopped fresh coriander. In a small bowl combine 2 tablespoons natural rice vinegar, 1 teaspoon toasted sesame oil, 1 teaspoon soy sauce, ½ teaspoon sugar and a dash of chilli flakes. While whisking, drizzle in 60 ml olive oil until it thickens slightly. Pour dressing over romaine mixture; toss to coat.

Balsamic-Glazed Salmon over Spinach

Cook the spinach until it's just wilted to maintain its fresh flavour and bright green colour. You'll need to do it in two batches.

PREP TIME	FUNCTION	CLOSED POT TIME	TOTAL TIME	RELEASE
10 minutes	Pressure/Manual (High); Sauté (Normal)	10 minutes	20 minutes + 10 minutes sauté	Quick

SERVES: 4

- 400 g to 675 g wild-caught Pacific salmon
- 60 ml balsamic vinegar
- 1½ teaspoons herbes de Provence
- 1½ teaspoons sea salt
- ½ teaspoon black pepper
- 240 ml water
- 3 tablespoons butter
- 2 cloves garlic, minced
- 900 g baby spinach (four 225-g bags)

PREP

Preheat the grill on your oven. Move rack to 13cm below grill.

Cut the salmon in two pieces to fit in the Instant Pot® if necessary. Drizzle 1 tablespoon of the vinegar, the herbes de Provence, 1 teaspoon of the salt and the pepper over the flesh side of the salmon.

Pour the water in the pot. Place the trivet in the bottom of the pot. Place fish, flesh side up, on the trivet. Secure the lid on the pot. Close the pressure-release valve.

COOK

Select **MANUAL** and cook at high pressure for 2 minutes. When cooking is complete, use a quick release to depressurise. Press **CANCEL**. Gently lift out the trivet with the fish. Place fish on rimmed baking sheet.

Place 1 tablespoon of the butter on top of the fish (divide between pieces). Grill the fish for 1 minute or until herbs are lightly browned.

Meanwhile, pour liquid from pot. Select **SAUTÉ** and adjust to **NORMAL**. Add 1 tablespoon of the remaining butter to the pot. When melted, add half of the garlic, half of the spinach and ¼ teaspoon of the salt. Cook, stirring, until the spinach is just wilted. Use tongs or a slotted spoon to remove spinach from pot and arrange on a platter. Repeat with remaining butter, garlic, spinach and salt. Use tongs or a slotted spoon to remove spinach from pot and add to platter.

Add the remaining 3 tablespoons vinegar to the pot and reduce for about 2 minutes until a glaze that coats the back of a spoon is formed.

SERVE

Arrange salmon on spinach. Drizzle the glaze on the salmon and serve immediately.

Dr. Karen Lee blogs at DrKarenSLee.com.

Braised Salmon in Tomato-Caper Sauce

Serve this Mediterranean-style salmon with cooked rice or polenta and a crisp green salad.

PREP TIME	FUNCTION	CLOSED POT TIME	TOTAL TIME	RELEASE
25 minutes	Sauté (Normal); Pressure/Manual (High)	20 minutes	45 minutes	Quick

SERVES: 4

- 1 tablespoon olive oil
- 2 shallots, finely chopped
- 1 red pepper, chopped
- 120 ml white wine
- 1 800-g tin whole tomatoes, undrained and cut up
- 1 tablespoon capers
- 1 teaspoon dried oregano, crushed
- ½ teaspoon dried thyme, crushed
- ½ teaspoon chilli flakes
- 4 115 g salmon fillets
- ¼ teaspoon salt
- ¼ teaspoon black pepper
- Cooked rice (optional)
- 1½ teaspoons chopped fresh flat-leaf parsley

PREP

Select **SAUTÉ** on the Instant Pot® and adjust to **NORMAL**. Add olive oil to pot. When the oil is hot, add shallots and red pepper. Cook, stirring occasionally, until shallots and pepper are just softened for about 3 minutes. Add white wine. Simmer for 2 minutes. Stir in tomatoes, capers, oregano, thyme and chilli flakes. Press **CANCEL**. Place salmon fillets in sauce. Sprinkle with salt and pepper. Secure the lid on the pot. Close the pressure-release valve.

COOK

Select **MANUAL** and cook at high pressure for 3 minutes. When cooking is complete, use a quick release to depressurise.

SERVE

If desired, serve with cooked rice. Top with parsley before serving.

Sole en Papillote

Cooking *en papillote*, or in parchment, is a classic French technique. It is particularly suited to delicate foods such as fish and vegetables. It's a wonderful way to infuse foods with flavour, retaining natural juices.

PREP TIME	FUNCTION	CLOSED POT TIME	TOTAL TIME	RELEASE
20 minutes	Pressure/Manual (Low)	15 minutes	35 minutes	Quick

SERVES: 2

- 240 ml water
- 175 ml matchstick-cut courgette
- 85 g matchstick-cut yellow pepper
- 50 g chopped tomatoes
- 1 clove garlic, minced
- 2 teaspoons olive oil
- ¼ teaspoon salt
- ⅛ teaspoon chilli flakes
- 2 115-g to 150 g fresh sole or tilapia fillets
- 2 sprigs fresh thyme
- 1 tablespoon butter
- ½ teaspoon lemon zest
- 2 tablespoons dry white wine
- Lemon wedges

PREP

Place trivet in Instant Pot®. Add the water to the pot.

In a medium bowl combine courgette, yellow pepper, tomatoes, garlic, olive oil, ⅛ teaspoon of the salt and the chilli flakes. Divide courgette mixture between two 35-cm squares of baking parchment, placing mixture to one side of parchment; top with fillets. Sprinkle fish with remaining ⅛ teaspoon salt.

Top each fillet with a sprig of thyme, half of the butter, ¼ teaspoon of the lemon zest and 1 tablespoon of the wine. For each package, fold parchment over fish and vegetables; fold the open sides in several times to secure, curving the edge into a circular pattern to seal. Place packets on trivet. Secure the lid on the pot. Close the pressure-release valve.

COOK

Select **MANUAL** and cook on low pressure for 7 minutes. When cooking is complete, use a quick release to depressurise.

SERVE

Place each package on a serving plate. Cut open with kitchen scissors. Serve with lemon wedges.

Asian-Style Steamed Fish & Vegetables

You can use any white fish you like–tilapia, cod, halibut or sea bass–in this super light and healthy veggie-packed dish.

PREP TIME	FUNCTION	CLOSED POT TIME	TOTAL TIME	RELEASE
40 minutes	Rice; Steam	30 minutes	1 hour 10 minutes	Quick

SERVES: 4

- 450 g fresh or frozen skinless tilapia, cod or other thin white fish fillets (about 1 cm thick)
- 225 g jasmine or basmati rice
- 240 ml water
- ½ teaspoon salt
- 2 spring onions
- 80 ml water
- 3 tablespoons reduced-salt soy sauce
- 1 tablespoon minced fresh ginger
- 2 teaspoons fish sauce (optional)
- 1 teaspoon sriracha sauce
- ¼ teaspoon black pepper
- 2 heads baby bok choy, halved lengthwise
- 75 g matchstick-cut carrots
- 1 tablespoon toasted sesame oil
- 1 tablespoon honey
- 2 teaspoons white and/or black sesame seeds, lightly toasted

PREP

Thaw fish, if frozen; set aside. Add rice, the 240 ml water and ¼ teaspoon of the salt to the Instant Pot®. Secure the lid on the pot. Close the pressure-release valve. Select **RICE**. When cooking is complete, use a quick release to depressurise. Transfer rice to a medium bowl; cover to keep warm.

Meanwhile, thinly slice spring onions, keeping white bottoms separate from green tops. In a small bowl whisk together the water, soy sauce, ginger, fish sauce (if using) and sriracha. Stir in sliced white bottoms of green onions. Reserve green tops.

Add ginger mixture to the pot after removing the rice. Press **CANCEL**. Place the trivet in the bottom of the pot. If necessary, cut fish into four serving-size pieces. Rinse fish; pat dry with kitchen paper. Sprinkle fish with remaining ¼ teaspoon salt and the pepper. Stack fish fillets in even layers on trivet in the pot. Top with bok choy and carrots. Secure the lid on the pot. Close the pressure-release valve.

COOK

Select **STEAM** and cook for 3 minutes. When cooking is complete, use a quick release to depressurise.

SERVE

Transfer carrots and bok choy to a platter. Lift trivet from the pot; transfer fish to the platter. Cover to keep warm. Add oil and honey to liquid in pot. Whisk until well combined.

Stir spring onion tops and sesame seeds into cooked rice. Divide rice, fish and vegetables among plates. Drizzle all with cooking liquid from pot.

Super-Quick Tuna & Noodles

Sometimes you just want rich, cheesy comfort food. Maybe it's a cold, rainy day – or maybe it's just been a not-very-good day. This family favourite will make everything good again.

PREP TIME	FUNCTION	CLOSED POT TIME	TOTAL TIME	RELEASE
5 minutes	Pressure/Manual (High)	25 minutes	30 minutes	Quick

SERVES: 6

1	450-g packet egg noodles
710	ml water
1	350-g tin tuna, drained
150	g frozen peas
3	300-g tin cream of mushroom soup
115	g grated cheddar cheese
15	g breadcrumbs (optional)

PREP
Place the noodles in the Instant Pot® and cover with the water. Place the tuna, peas and soup on top of the pasta. Secure the lid on the pot. Close the pressure-release valve.

COOK
Select **MANUAL** and cook at high pressure for 4 minutes. When cooking is complete, use a quick release to depressurise.

SERVE
Stir in the cheese. If desired, place the mixture in a baking dish and cover with breadcrumbs. Place under the grill for 2 to 3 minutes.

 Carla Bushey blogs at AdventuresofaNurse.com.

Citrus Prawns with Orange-Cashew Rice

Prawns look a bit like a cross between a prawn and a lobster and have sweet, delicately flavoured meat. If you can't find them, jumbo prawns will work perfectly well in this dish.

PREP TIME	FUNCTION	CLOSED POT TIME	TOTAL TIME	RELEASE
40 minutes	Rice; Pressure/Manual (High)	40 minutes	30 minutes + 1 hour marinate	Natural/Quick

SERVES: 4

PRAWNS

- 60 ml vegetable oil
- 1 tablespoon Dijon mustard
- 3 cloves garlic, minced
- Juice from 1 lemon (3 to 4 tablespoons)
- Juice from 1 lime (2 to 3 tablespoons)
- Juice from 2 oranges (about 120 ml)
- 20 large or jumbo prawns, peeled and deveined

ORANGE-CASHEW RICE

- 335 g long grain rice
- 475 ml water
- 2 teaspoons orange zest
- Juice from 1 orange (about 60 ml)
- ¼ teaspoon salt
- 110 g roasted salted cashew halves

PREP

For prawns, in a resealable plastic bag combine oil, mustard, garlic, lemon juice, lime juice and orange juice. Shake well to mix. Add prawns; gently shake bag to coat all prawns with marinade. Transfer bag to fridge; let prawns marinate for 1 hour.

When prawns have marinated for about 25 minutes, prepare Orange-Cashew Rice: Combine rice, the water, orange zest, orange juice and salt in the Instant Pot®. Secure the lid on the pot. Close the pressure-release valve.

COOK

Select **RICE**. When cooking is complete, use a natural release to depressurise. Transfer cooked rice to a bowl. Stir in cashews. Cover to keep warm.

Place the trivet in the pot. Arrange prawns on trivet. Pour the marinade in the pot up to, but not touching, the prawns; discard extra marinade. Secure the lid on the pot. Close the pressure-release valve. Press **CANCEL**.

Select **MANUAL** and cook at high pressure for 1 minute. When cooking is complete, use a quick release to depressurise.

SERVE

Serve prawns on top of Orange-Cashew Rice; drizzle with hot marinade from pot.

Spicy Prawns with Grits & Bacon

The jalapeño contributes most of the heat to this dish. Poblano peppers are generally fairly mild – although they can vary a bit in their heat level – and have a mellow, fruity flavour.

PREP TIME	FUNCTION		CLOSED POT TIME	TOTAL TIME	RELEASE
30 minutes	Pressure/Manual (High); Sauté (Normal)		30 minutes	1 hour	Natural

SERVES: 4

450 g fresh or frozen peeled and deveined jumbo prawns (15 prawns)

175 ml water

110 g coarsely ground polenta

240 ml reduced-salt chicken stock

240 ml whipping cream

3 cloves garlic, minced

¼ teaspoon salt

⅛ teaspoon black pepper

240 ml water

4 slices bacon, chopped

1 medium poblano pepper, cut into thin bite-size strips

75 g chopped red onion

1 small jalapeño pepper, finely chopped

1 tablespoon cider vinegar (optional)

PREP

Thaw prawns if frozen. Set aside. For grits, in a 1.5-litre round ceramic or glass round casserole (make sure the dish will fit down into the Instant Pot® first), stir together the 175 ml water, polenta, stock, cream, garlic, salt and black pepper. Tear an 45-cm-long sheet of foil. Fold the sheet lengthwise into thirds to make a long, narrow sling.

Place the trivet in bottom of the pot. Add the 240 ml water. Place filled casserole in the centre of the foil sling. Use the sling to lower the casserole into the pot until it sits on the trivet. Tuck foil into pot so the lid will go on. Secure the lid on the pot. Close the pressure-release valve.

COOK

Select **MANUAL** and cook at high pressure for 10 minutes. When cooking is complete, use a natural release to depressurise. Press **CANCEL**. Lift the casserole out of the pot using the foil sling. Cover casserole loosely to keep warm.

Meanwhile, rinse prawns with cold water; pat dry with kitchen paper. Carefully remove the trivet from pot and pour out the water. Select **SAUTÉ** and adjust to **NORMAL**. When hot, add bacon. Cook for 3 to 4 minutes. Add poblano pepper, onion and jalapeño. Cook for 5 to 7 minutes or until bacon is browned and vegetables are just tender, stirring occasionally. Using a slotted spoon, transfer bacon mixture to a medium bowl; set aside.

Cook prawns in bacon drippings in pot for 4 minutes or until prawns are opaque, turning once halfway through cooking. If desired, add vinegar to bacon mixture; toss to coat. Add all prawns and the bacon mixture to the pot; toss gently to combine. Press **CANCEL**.

SERVE

To serve, divide grits among shallow bowls. Top evenly with prawn mixture.

Spicy Scallops with Tomatoes over Couscous

Israeli couscous is also called pearl couscous. It is larger than fine-grained Moroccan-style couscous and has a wonderfully toothsome, chewy texture when cooked.

PREP TIME	FUNCTION	CLOSED POT TIME	TOTAL TIME	RELEASE
20 minutes	Sauté (Normal); Pressure/Manual (High)	10 minutes	30 minutes	Quick

SERVES: 4

- 450 g sea scallops
- Kosher salt
- Black pepper
- 2 tablespoons olive oil
- 2 cloves garlic, minced
- 1 300-g tin diced tomatoes with green chillis
- 1 225-g tin tomato sauce
- 2 tablespoons fresh lime juice
- 620 g hot cooked Israeli couscous
- 1 jalapeño pepper, thinly sliced
- 2 tablespoons chopped fresh coriander
- 2 tablespoons sliced spring onion

PREP

Pat the scallops dry and lightly season with salt and black pepper.

Select **SAUTÉ** on the Instant Pot® and adjust to **NORMAL**. Add olive oil. When oil is hot, add scallops and garlic. Cook scallops, without moving, for 1 minute or just until golden brown on bottom. Turn scallops over and repeat. (The scallops will not be cooked through at this point.) Press **CANCEL**.

Add the tomatoes and tomato sauce to the pot. Secure the lid on the pot. Close the pressure-release valve.

COOK

Select **MANUAL** and cook at high pressure for 1 minute. When cooking is complete, use a quick release to depressurise.

SERVE

Stir in lime juice. Serve the scallops and cooking liquid over the couscous. Top with jalapeño slices, coriander and spring onion.

Beer-Buzzed Mussels

Mussels are tender and taste delightfully of the sea, but the real draw is the flavourful cooking liquid – which is drizzled over the mussels and mopped up with toasted baguette. Yum!

PREP TIME	FUNCTION	CLOSED POT TIME	TOTAL TIME	RELEASE
30 minutes	Sauté (Normal); Steam	20 minutes	50 minutes	Quick

SERVES: 2 or 3 as a main dish; 4 to 6 as an appetizer

- 2 tablespoons butter
- 1 tablespoon minced garlic
- ½ teaspoon chilli flakes
- ½ teaspoon black pepper
- 2 sprigs fresh thyme
- 1 bay leaf
- 1 350-ml bottle beer
- 900 g mussels, scrubbed and debearded*
- 15 g chopped flat-leaf parsley
- Lemon wedges (optional)
- Toasted baguette slices (optional)

PREP

Select **SAUTÉ** on the Instant Pot® and adjust to **NORMAL**. Add butter to pot. When butter is melted, add garlic and chilli flakes. Cook and stir over medium heat for 1 minute or until garlic is fragrant but not browned. Press **CANCEL**. Add black pepper, thyme, bay leaf and beer; stir to combine. Add mussels to pot. Secure the lid on the pot. Close the pressure-release valve.

COOK

Select **STEAM** and cook for 3 minutes. When cooking is complete, use a quick release to depressurise.

SERVE

Transfer mussels to serving bowls. Remove and discard bay leaf. Ladle with steaming liquid. Sprinkle with chopped parsley. If desired, garnish with lemon wedges and serve with toasted baguette slices for dipping.

*__TIP:__ Cook mussels the day they are purchased. If using wild-harvested mussels, soak in a bowl of cold water for 20 minutes to help flush out grit and sand. (This is not necessary for farm-raised mussels.) Using a stiff brush, scrub mussels, one at a time, under cold running water. Debeard mussels about 10 to 15 minutes before cooking. The beard is the small cluster of fibres that emerges from the shell. To remove the beards, grasp the string between your thumb and forefinger and pull towards the hinge. You can also use pliers or fish tweezers. Be sure that the shell of each mussel is tightly closed. If any shells are open, tap them gently. Discard any mussels that don't close within a few minutes. Discard any mussels with cracked or damaged shells.

Mussels Frites

It doesn't get more French than this bistro-style favourite – mussels steamed in garlic-infused white wine and served with herbed fries and flavoured mayonnaise for dipping.

PREP TIME	FUNCTION		CLOSED POT TIME	TOTAL TIME	RELEASE
30 minutes	Manual/Pressure (High)		20 minutes	50 minutes	Quick

SERVES: 4 to 6

FRITES

- 1 tablespoon chopped fresh rosemary
- 1½ teaspoons garlic powder
- 1 teaspoon salt
- ¾ teaspoon black pepper
- 675 g russet or gold potatoes, cut into 1-cm-thick sticks
- 3 tablespoons olive oil

MUSSELS

- 240 ml white wine
- 3 roma tomatoes, seeded and chopped
- 2 cloves garlic, minced
- 1 bay leaf
- 900 g mussels, scrubbed and debearded (see Tip, page 137)
- 1 tablespoon chopped fresh flat-leaf parsley

DIPPING SAUCE

- 75 g mayonnaise
- 2 tablespoons minced roasted red pepper
- 1 clove garlic, minced

PREP

Preheat oven to 230°C/450°F. In a small bowl combine rosemary, garlic powder, salt and pepper. On a large baking sheet or roasting tin toss the potatoes with the olive oil and spice mixture. Roast for 25 to 30 minutes or until tender and browned, stirring once.

Combine the wine, tomatoes, garlic and bay leaf in the Instant Pot®. Top with the mussels. Secure the lid on the pot. Close the pressure-release valve.

COOK

Select **MANUAL** and cook at high pressure for 3 minutes. When cooking is complete, use a quick release to depressurise.

SERVE

Meanwhile, for the dipping sauce, in a small bowl combine the mayonnaise, roasted red pepper and garlic.

Top mussels with parsley. Serve the frites with the dipping sauce alongside the mussels.

Steamed Lobster Tail with Meunière Sauce

Rich, meaty lobster tail doesn't need a lot of embellishment. This classic French sauce of browned butter, lemon, parsley and capers is just right.

PREP TIME	FUNCTION		CLOSED POT TIME	TOTAL TIME	RELEASE
10 minutes	Steam		10 minutes	20 minutes	Quick

SERVES: 2

- 120 ml water
- 120 ml white wine
- 1 to 2 fresh thyme sprig(s)
- 2 garlic cloves, sliced
- 2 small (115 g) lobster tails, cut in half from top to tail
- 55 g unsalted butter
- 2 tablespoons fresh lemon juice
- 2 tablespoons chopped fresh flat-leaf parsley
- 1 tablespoon capers, drained and minced

PREP

Place the trivet in the pot. Place the water, wine, thyme and garlic in the Instant Pot®. Place tails, shell sides down, on trivet. Secure the lid on the pot. Close the pressure-release valve.

COOK

Select **STEAM** and cook for 2 minutes. When cooking is complete, use a quick release to depressurise.

SERVE

While tails are steaming, heat butter over medium-high heat in a frying pan until golden brown for about 3 to 5 minutes. Remove from heat and carefully stir in lemon juice, parsley and capers. (Careful: hot butter may splatter.) Keep warm until tails are ready.

Drizzle sauce over tails or pour in a dish for dipping.

Beans & Grains

No-Fry Refried Beans

There's no frying – and no soaking – required to make these creamy, Mexican-style pinto beans. Serve them as a side to tacos, burritos or quesadillas or with hot cooked rice as a main dish.

PREP TIME	FUNCTION	CLOSED POT TIME	TOTAL TIME	RELEASE
20 minutes	Pressure/Manual (High); Sauté (Normal)	1 hour 20 minutes	1 hour 40 minutes	Natural

SERVES: 6 to 8

- 300 g dried pinto beans
- 1.4 litres reduced-salt chicken stock
- 4 to 6 sprigs fresh coriander
- ¾ teaspoon ground cumin
- 1 bay leaf (optional)
- 1 tablespoon vegetable oil
- 75 g chopped onion
- 1 small jalapeño pepper, finely chopped
- 3 cloves garlic, minced
- 2 tablespoons chopped fresh coriander
- 1 teaspoon chopped fresh oregano or ¼ teaspoon dried oregano, crushed
- Salt and freshly ground black pepper

PREP

Rinse beans with cold water and pick through the beans to remove any pebbles or discoloured or shriveled beans. Add the beans to the Instant Pot®. Add stock, coriander, ½ teaspoon of the cumin and, if desired, the bay leaf. Secure the lid on the pot. Close the pressure-release valve.

COOK

Select **MANUAL** and cook on high pressure for 40 minutes. When cooking is complete, use a natural release to depressurise. Press **CANCEL**.

Pour beans into a heatproof colander set over a large bowl to catch the cooking liquid. Remove and discard bay leaf (if using) and coriander sprigs. Set beans and liquid aside.

Select **SAUTÉ** on the pot and adjust to **NORMAL**. When hot, add the oil to the pot. Add the onion, jalapeño and garlic. Cook for 3 minutes or until tender, stirring occasionally. Press **CANCEL**. Stir in remaining ¼ teaspoon cumin. Return drained beans to pot with onion mixture. Add 360 ml of the reserved bean cooking liquid.

SERVE

Using a potato masher or immersion blender, mash or blend beans to desired consistency, adding additional bean cooking liquid as needed. Stir in chopped coriander and oregano.

Season to taste with salt and black pepper.

Cajun Red Beans & Rice

Rice and beans is a hearty, filling – and highly economical – combo enjoyed all over the world. With the switch of the type of legume, the seasonings and other ingredients, it becomes a completely different dish.

PREP TIME	FUNCTION	CLOSED POT TIME	TOTAL TIME	RELEASE
25 minutes	Sauté (Normal); Bean/Chili (Normal)	1 hour 25 minutes	1 hour 50 minutes + overnight soak	Natural

SERVES: 6 to 8

450 g dried red kidney beans

2 tablespoons olive oil

450 g spicy chorizo sausage, sliced

1 onion, chopped

1 green pepper, chopped

2 stalks celery, chopped

1 jalapeño pepper, seeded (if desired) and finely chopped

3 cloves garlic, minced

950 ml reduced-salt chicken stock

2 bay leaves

2 teaspoons Cajun seasoning

½ teaspoon black pepper

½ teaspoon dried thyme, crushed

½ teaspoon dried sage, crushed

Cooked white rice

PREP

Soak beans in water to cover overnight. Rinse and drain.

Select **SAUTÉ** on the Instant Pot® and adjust to **NORMAL**. Add olive oil. When oil is hot, add the sausage and cook for 5 minutes or until browned. Add the onion, sweet pepper, celery, jalapeño and garlic. Cook and stir until vegetables are softened for about 3 minutes. Press **CANCEL**.

Add the beans, stock, bay leaves, Cajun seasoning, black pepper, thyme and sage. Secure the lid on the pot. Close the pressure-release valve.

COOK

Select **BEAN/CHILI*** and adjust to **NORMAL**. When cooking is complete, use a natural release to depressurise.

SERVE

Remove and discard bay leaves. Serve with cooked white rice.

*TIP: If your Instant Pot® doesn't have a **BEAN/CHILI** button, select **MANUAL** and cook for 30 minutes at high pressure.

Caribbean Rice & Beans

In this island-inspired dish, the rice and beans are stirred together. To make it vegetarian (even vegan!), use vegetable stock in place of the chicken stock.

PREP TIME	FUNCTION		CLOSED POT TIME	TOTAL TIME	RELEASE
15 minutes	Sauté (Normal); Rice		35 minutes	50 minutes	Natural

SERVES: 4 as a main dish; 8 as a side dish

- 2 tablespoons vegetable oil
- 1 onion, chopped
- 3 cloves garlic, minced
- 1 tablespoon minced fresh ginger
- 480 ml reduced-salt chicken stock
- 125 g cooked black beans or red beans or two 425-g tins black beans or red beans, drained and rinsed
- 335 g long grain white rice, rinsed and drained
- 240 ml tinned coconut milk (full fat)
- 1 whole Scotch bonnet or habanero pepper, pricked with a fork
- 2 sprigs fresh thyme or ½ teaspoon dried thyme, crushed
- ½ teaspoon salt
- ¼ teaspoon ground allspice
- 1 tablespoon chopped fresh coriander or parsley

PREP
Select **SAUTÉ** on the Instant Pot® and adjust to **NORMAL**. Add oil to pot. When oil is hot, add the onion. Cook and stir until onion is softened for about 3 minutes. Add garlic and ginger. Cook for 2 minutes more, stirring occasionally. Press **CANCEL**. Stir in chicken stock, beans, rice, coconut milk, Scotch bonnet, thyme, salt and allspice. Secure the lid on the pot. Close the pressure-release valve.

COOK
Select **RICE**. When cooking is complete, use a natural release to depressurise.

SERVE
Remove and discard whole Scotch bonnet pepper and, if using, thyme sprigs. Top each serving with chopped coriander.

Cuban Black Beans & Rice

If you forgot to soak the beans overnight, you can use the quick-soak method: Place beans in a large pot and cover with water by 5 cm. Bring to a boil and let boil for 1 minute. Remove from heat and let the beans stand, covered, for 1 hour. Drain, rinse and proceed with the recipe.

PREP TIME	FUNCTION	CLOSED POT TIME	TOTAL TIME	RELEASE
25 minutes	Sauté (Normal); Pressure/Manual (High)	1 hour 35 minutes	2 hours + overnight soak	Natural

SERVES: 6 to 8

- 450 g dried black beans
- 2 tablespoons olive oil
- 1 large onion, chopped
- 1 red pepper, chopped
- 1 green pepper, chopped
- 1 jalapeño pepper, seeded (if desired) and finely chopped
- 2 cloves garlic, minced
- 950 ml chicken stock
- 1 large smoked ham hock or 2 small smoked ham hocks
- 2 Roma tomatoes, seeded and chopped
- 2 bay leaves
- 1 teaspoon dried oregano
- 1 teaspoon ground cumin
- 1 teaspoon paprika
- 1 teaspoon salt
- ½ teaspoon black pepper
- Lime wedges
- Cooked white rice
- Fresh coriander leaves

PREP

Soak beans in water to cover overnight. Rinse and drain.

Select **SAUTÉ** on the Instant Pot® and adjust to **NORMAL**. Add olive oil. When oil is hot, add the onion, peppers, jalapeño and garlic. Cook and stir until vegetables are softened for about 5 minutes. Press **CANCEL**. Add the beans, stock, ham hock(s), tomatoes, bay leaves, oregano, cumin, paprika, salt and black pepper. Secure the lid on the pot. Close the pressure-release valve.

COOK

Select **MANUAL** and cook at high pressure for 45 minutes. When cooking is complete, use a natural release to depressurise.

Remove ham hock(s); let cool slightly. Remove and discard bay leaves. Mash bean mixture with a potato masher to desired consistency. When the ham hock is cool enough to handle, remove meat; chop. Stir the meat into the beans.

SERVE

Serve with lime wedges over cooked white rice. Top with coriander.

Ham & Sweetcorn Risotto

This recipe may call for high-starch Arborio rice–the standard for the Italian dish–but the ingredients and flavourings are all-American. Try it with fresh corn during sweetcorn season.

PREP TIME	FUNCTION	CLOSED POT TIME	TOTAL TIME	RELEASE
20 minutes	Sauté (Normal); Manual/Pressure (High)	25 minutes	45 minutes + 10 minutes stand	Quick

SERVES: 6

- 2 tablespoons olive oil
- 1 large shallot, finely chopped
- 335 g Arborio rice
- 2 cloves garlic, minced
- 240 ml dry white wine
- ½ teaspoon salt
- ¼ teaspoon freshly ground black pepper
- 1.4 litres chicken stock
- 350 g fresh sweet corn kernels or 350 g frozen corn, thawed
- 150 g chopped ham
- 115 g grated chilli cheddar
- 2 tablespoons snipped fresh dill

PREP

Select **SAUTÉ** on the Instant Pot® and adjust to **NORMAL**. Add oil to pot. When oil is hot, add shallot and rice. Cook and stir for 5 minutes or until rice looks translucent. Stir in garlic and wine; cook and stir 2 to 3 minutes or until wine is absorbed. Press **CANCEL**.

Add salt, pepper, stock, corn and ham. Secure the lid on the pot. Close the pressure-release valve.

COOK

Select **MANUAL** and cook at high pressure for 8 minutes. When cooking is complete, use a quick release to depressurise.

SERVE

Stir the risotto until any surface liquid disappears, then stir in cheese. Let stand for 10 minutes before serving. Garnish each serving with dill.

Mushroom & Spinach Risotto

The traditional cooking method for risotto involves standing at the hob and stirring almost constantly to achieve the signature creamy texture of the dish. The Instant Pot® eliminates that, turning out luscious risotto with the touch of a button.

PREP TIME	FUNCTION	CLOSED POT TIME	TOTAL TIME	RELEASE
25 minutes	Sauté (Normal); Pressure/Manual (High)	20 minutes	45 minutes	Quick

SERVES: 4

- 2 tablespoons olive oil
- 50 g chopped shallots
- 1 225-g packet cremini mushrooms, sliced
- ¼ teaspoon salt
- ⅛ teaspoon chilli flakes
- 2 cloves garlic, minced
- 480 ml chicken or vegetable stock
- 225 g Arborio rice
- ¼ teaspoon dried thyme
- 1 tablespoon butter
- 100 g baby spinach
- 35 g freshly grated Parmesan cheese

PREP

Select **SAUTÉ** on the Instant Pot® and adjust to **NORMAL**. Add oil to pot. When oil is hot, add shallots and cook for 2 minutes to soften, stirring occasionally. Add mushrooms, salt and chilli flakes; cook for 4 minutes or until mushrooms are tender, stirring frequently. Add garlic; cook and stir for 1 minute more. Press **CANCEL**. Add stock, rice and thyme. Secure the lid on the pot. Close the pressure-release valve.

COOK

Select **MANUAL** and cook at high pressure for 6 minutes. When cooking is complete, use a quick release to depressurise.

SERVE

Add butter and spinach to rice mixture; stir to wilt spinach. Stir in Parmesan cheese.

Wild Rice-Blueberry Pilaf

Two Northwoods ingredients come together in this earthy pilaf. Try it with roast turkey or chicken.

PREP TIME	FUNCTION	CLOSED POT TIME	TOTAL TIME	RELEASE
15 minutes	Sauté (Normal); Pressure/Manual (High)	45 minutes	1 hour	Natural

SERVES: 6 to 8

3	tablespoons butter
50	g finely chopped red onion
225	g wild rice
225	g long grain brown rice
710	ml chicken stock
2	teaspoons fresh thyme leaves
½	teaspoon salt
¼	teaspoon black pepper
40	g toasted, coarsely chopped pecans
60	g dried blueberries
1½	teaspoons chopped fresh flat-leaf parsley

PREP

Select **SAUTÉ** on the Instant Pot® and adjust to **NORMAL**. Add butter to pot. When melted, add onion. Cook onion, stirring constantly until softened for about 2 to 3 minutes. Add wild rice and brown rice; cook and stir for 4 to 5 minutes or until rice toasts. Press **CANCEL**. Add stock, thyme, salt and pepper.

Secure the lid on the pot. Close the pressure-release valve.

COOK

Select **MANUAL** and cook at high pressure for 25 minutes. When cooking is complete, use a natural release to depressurise.

SERVE

Add pecans, blueberries and parsley; toss well. Serve immediately.

Greek Quinoa, Chickpea & Lettuce Wraps

Although most quinoa is sold pre-rinsed, it's not a bad idea to rinse it again, just in case. In their natural state, the grains are coated with a bitter substance called saponin that is thought to ward off birds and other creatures that might want to munch on them.

PREP TIME	FUNCTION	CLOSED POT TIME	TOTAL TIME	RELEASE
30 minutes	Pressure/Manual (High)	15 minutes	45 minutes + 5 minutes cool	Quick

SERVES: 4

- 240 ml water
- 120 g dried tricolor quinoa, rinsed and drained
- ½ teaspoon salt
- 1 425-g tin garbanzo beans, rinsed and drained
- 150 g thinly sliced cucumber
- 1 small red pepper, cut into thin strips
- 50 g thinly sliced spring onions
- 80 ml olive oil
- 80 ml lemon juice
- 1 tablespoon chopped fresh mint
- ¼ teaspoon freshly ground black pepper
- 12 round lettuce leaves
- 60 g feta cheese
- 35 g pine nuts, toasted

PREP
Combine the water, quinoa and salt in the Instant Pot®; stir to combine. Secure the lid on the pot. Close the pressure-release valve.

COOK
Select **MANUAL** and cook at high pressure for 2 minutes. Once cooking is complete, use a quick release to depressurise.

Drain off liquid if needed. Spread cooked quinoa in a shallow tin and let cool for 5 minutes before using.

SERVE
Transfer cooled quinoa to a large bowl. Add beans, cucumber, pepper and spring onions.

In a small bowl whisk together oil, lemon juice, mint and black pepper. Pour over quinoa mixture; toss gently until well combined.

Divide lettuce leaves among four plates, placing them bowl sides up. Spoon quinoa mixture evenly onto lettuce leaves. Sprinkle with feta cheese and pine nuts.

Wheat Berry Pilaf with Kalamata Olives

Wheat berries have a delightfully chewy texture and nutty flavour. Tossed with garlic, sautéed mushrooms, soy sauce, white wine, herbs, lemon and meaty Kalamata olives, they become a savoury side to beef or lamb.

PREP TIME	FUNCTION	CLOSED POT TIME	TOTAL TIME	RELEASE
5 minutes	Pressure/Manual (High); Sauté (Normal)	1 hour 10 minutes	1 hour 15 minutes + 10 minutes	Natural

SERVES: 4 to 6

- 120 g uncooked wheat berries
- 950 ml water
- 1 tablespoon olive oil
- 1 small onion, chopped
- ½ teaspoon salt
- 1 tablespoon butter
- 4 cloves garlic, minced
- 225 g mushrooms, sliced
- 1 tablespoon soy sauce
- 60 ml dry white wine
- 60 ml chicken stock
- ½ teaspoon snipped fresh thyme
- 1 teaspoon snipped fresh rosemary
- 1 teaspoon lemon zest
- 50 g pitted Kalamata olives, sliced
- Black pepper

PREP

Combine wheat berries and the water in the Instant Pot®. Secure the lid on the pot. Close the pressure-release valve.

COOK

Select **MANUAL** and cook at high pressure for 35 minutes. When cooking is complete, use a natural release to depressurise. Press **CANCEL**.

Drain wheat berries in a fine-mesh strainer and set aside. Wipe inner pot dry and replace.

Select **SAUTÉ** and adjust to **NORMAL**. Add oil to pot. When oil is hot, add onion and salt. Cook and stir until onion is softened for about 4 to 5 minutes. Add butter, garlic, mushrooms and soy sauce and continue cooking for 5 to 7 minutes until mushrooms release their liquid. Add wine and chicken stock and simmer for about 3 minutes until liquid begins to evaporate. Add cooked wheat berries, thyme, rosemary, lemon zest and olives. Heat through, stirring occasionally. Press **CANCEL**.

SERVE

Season to taste with pepper and additional salt.

Kale, Farro & Feta

Farro is the Italian name for emmer wheat, an ancient variety of hard wheat. It comes whole, semi-pearled and pearled. Whole farro retains all of the bran. It has the most fibre but takes the longest time to cook. Semi-pearled has some of the bran removed and pearled has all of it removed. It cooks the most quickly – especially in the Instant Pot®.

PREP TIME	FUNCTION		CLOSED POT TIME	TOTAL TIME	RELEASE
10 minutes	Sauté (Normal); Pressure/Manual (High)		40 minutes	50 minutes	Natural

SERVES: 6 to 8

- 200 g pearled farro
- 1 tablespoon olive oil
- 1.8 kg chopped kale (about 1 large bunch)
- 360 ml reduced-salt chicken stock or vegetable stock
- 1 tablespoon fresh lemon juice
- ¼ teaspoon salt
- ¼ teaspoon black pepper
- 40 g crumbled feta cheese
- 25 g toasted almond slices

PREP

Rinse farro under running water. Set aside. Select **SAUTÉ** on the Instant Pot® and adjust to **NORMAL**. When hot, add the oil and chopped kale. Cook for 2 minutes, stirring often. Press **CANCEL**. Place farro and stock in the pot. Secure the lid on the pot. Close the pressure-release valve.

COOK

Select **MANUAL** and cook at high pressure for 25 minutes. When cooking is complete, use a natural release to depressurise.

SERVE

Stir in lemon juice, salt and pepper. Spoon mixture into a serving bowl. Top with feta and almonds. Serve immediately.

Thai Quinoa Salad

While the quinoa is cooking and cooling, prep the rest of the ingredients for this fresh and light veggie-packed salad that can be on the table in 30 minutes.

PREP TIME	FUNCTION	CLOSED POT TIME	TOTAL TIME	RELEASE
5 minutes	Pressure/Manual (High)	15 minutes	30 minutes + 5 minutes cool	Quick

SERVES: 4 to 6

225 g quinoa, rinsed and drained

480 ml water

⅛ teaspoon salt

60 ml fresh lime juice

60 ml untoasted sesame oil

1 tablespoon soy sauce

1 teaspoon sugar

⅛ teaspoon to ¼ teaspoon chilli flakes

1 small clove garlic, minced

2 tablespoons chopped spring onions (green part only)

100 g lettuce or baby spinach leaves

1 medium seedless cucumber, thinly sliced on the diagonal

2 medium carrots, thinly sliced on the diagonal

250 g leftover shredded chicken

1 tablespoon fresh basil leaves

1 tablespoon fresh mint leaves

60 g peanuts, coarsely chopped

Lime wedges

PREP

Combine quinoa, the water and salt in the Instant Pot®. Secure the lid on the pot. Close the pressure-release valve.

COOK

Select **MANUAL** and cook at high pressure for 2 minutes. When cooking is complete, use a quick release to depressurise.

While quinoa is cooking, make the dressing: combine lime juice, sesame oil, soy sauce, sugar, chilli flakes, garlic and spring onions in a small bowl. Whisk until the sugar dissolves.

Spread cooked quinoa in a shallow pan and let cool for 5 minutes before using.

SERVE

In a large bowl combine quinoa, lettuce, cucumber, carrots and chicken. Drizzle with the dressing. Toss gently to coat. Top with basil, mint leaves and peanuts. Serve with lime wedges.

1-Minute Golden Pressure-Cooker Pilaf

Turmeric – prized by cooks for its earthy, pungent flavour and by naturopaths for its proven anti-inflammatory properties – gives this simple pilaf its beautiful golden colour.

PREP TIME	FUNCTION	CLOSED POT TIME	TOTAL TIME	RELEASE
5 minutes	Sauté (Normal); Pressure/Manual (High)	10 minutes	15 minutes	Natural

SERVES: 6

- 2 tablespoons olive oil
- 2 garlic cloves, smashed
- 2 teaspoons turmeric
- 2 teaspoons cumin
- 1 teaspoon salt
- 710 ml water
- 340 g quinoa, rinsed and drained*
- Chopped fresh mint, coriander, or curly-leaf parsley, for garnish (optional)

PREP

Select **SAUTÉ** on the Instant Pot® and adjust to **NORMAL**. When hot, add the oil and garlic. **SAUTÉ** for about 30 seconds. Press **CANCEL**. Stir in the turmeric, cumin and salt. Add the water and quinoa to the pot. Secure the lid on the pot. Close the pressure-release valve.

COOK

Select **MANUAL** and cook at high pressure for 1 minute. When cooking is complete, use a natural release to depressurise.

SERVE

Transfer quinoa to a serving bowl. Fluff with a fork. If desired, garnish with fresh herbs before serving.

***TIP:** Although most quinoa is pre-rinsed, it's a good step to take to ensure that the bitter natural coating called saponin is fully rinsed and rubbed off the grains.

Laura Pazzaglia blogs at HipPressureCooking.com.

Mexican Quinoa

Quinoa is high in protein and low in carbohydrate – making it an ideal health food. When it's combined with black beans, vegetables and Mexican seasonings – and topped with a little salty cheese – you won't even think about the fact that it's good for you.

PREP TIME	FUNCTION	CLOSED POT TIME	TOTAL TIME	RELEASE
25 minutes	Sauté (Normal); Pressure/Manual (High)	15 minutes	40 minutes	Quick

SERVES: 4

- 2 tablespoons olive oil
- 75 g coarsely chopped onion
- 80 g coarsely chopped yellow pepper
- 1 medium jalapeño pepper, seeded and finely chopped
- 2 cloves garlic, minced
- ½ teaspoon salt
- 425 ml chicken or vegetable stock
- 170 g uncooked white quinoa, rinsed and drained
- 1 425-g tin black beans, rinsed and drained
- 200 g coarsely chopped fresh tomato
- 1 tablespoon chilli powder
- 2 tablespoons chopped fresh coriander
- 125 g crumbled feta
- Lime wedges

PREP
Select **SAUTÉ** on the Instant Pot® and adjust to **NORMAL**. Heat oil in pot; add onion, pepper, jalapeño, garlic and salt. Cook for 3 to 5 minutes or until softened, stirring frequently. Press **CANCEL**. Add stock, quinoa, beans, tomato and chilli powder. Secure the lid on the pot. Close the pressure-release valve.

COOK
Select **MANUAL** and cook at high pressure for 2 minutes. When cooking is complete, use a quick release to depressurise.

SERVE
Stir coriander into quinoa mixture. Top with feta and serve with lime wedges.

Chickpea-Broccoli Salad

This colourful blend of chickpeas, broccoli, red onion and Kalamata olives dressed in a classic Dijon vinaigrette is the perfect dish to take on a picnic.

PREP TIME	FUNCTION	CLOSED POT TIME	TOTAL TIME	RELEASE
25 minutes	Pressure/Manual (High, Low)	35 minutes	1 hour	Natural/Quick

SERVES: 4

- 120 g dried chickpeas, soaked overnight and drained
- 3 cloves garlic, minced
- 240 ml vegetable stock
- 225 g broccoli florets or tenderstem broccoli
- 75 g sliced red onion
- 1½ teaspoons chopped fresh flat-leaf parsley
- 3 tablespoons chopped Kalamata olives (optional)
- ¼ teaspoon to ½ teaspoon chilli flakes

DRESSING

- 1 tablespoon fresh lemon juice
- 1 tablespoon red wine vinegar
- 2 teaspoon Dijon mustard
- 1 teaspoon minced fresh garlic
- 1 tablespoon extra virgin olive oil

PREP
Combine chickpeas, garlic and stock in the Instant Pot®. Secure the lid on the pot. Close the pressure-release valve.

COOK
Select **MANUAL** and cook at high pressure for 13 minutes. When cooking is complete, use a natural release to depressurise.

While the chickpeas cook, make the dressing: Whisk lemon juice, vinegar, mustard, garlic and olive oil in a medium bowl; set aside.

Add the broccoli to the pot. Secure the lid on the pot. Close the pressure-release valve. Select **MANUAL** and cook at low pressure for 1 minute. When cooking is complete, use a quick release to depressurise. (Alternatively, stir in the broccoli, secure the lid and let sit until the broccoli becomes tender.)

SERVE
Using a slotted spoon, transfer the contents to a serving bowl.

Combine the dressing with the chickpeas and broccoli. Add the onion, parsley, olives (if using) and chilli flakes; toss to coat.

Serve salad warm or chilled.

Jill Nussinow blogs at TheVeggieQueen.com and is the author of Vegan Under Pressure.

Vegetables

Light & Fluffy Mashed Potatoes

Go classic or with one of the fun variations – Cheesy Garlic or Sriracha-Ranch.

PREP TIME	FUNCTION	CLOSED POT TIME	TOTAL TIME	RELEASE
20 minutes	Pressure/Manual (High); Sauté (Less)	30 minutes	50 minutes	Natural

SERVES: 6 to 8

- 900 g russet or Yukon gold potatoes, peeled and cut into 5-cm to 7-cm pieces
- 480 ml reduced-salt chicken stock or water*
- ¼ teaspoon black pepper
- 120 ml milk
- 2 tablespoons butter
- Salt
- Chopped fresh chives (optional)
- Freshly ground black pepper (optional)

PREP
Combine potatoes, stock and pepper in the Instant Pot®. Secure the lid on the pot. Close the pressure-release valve.

COOK
Select **MANUAL** and cook at high pressure for 6 minutes. When cooking is complete, use a natural release to depressurise. Press **CANCEL**.

Carefully pour most of the liquid from the pot into a medium bowl; set aside. Add milk and butter to the potatoes in pot. Select **SAUTÉ** and adjust to **LESS**. Use a potato masher to mash potatoes to desired texture. Add reserved cooking liquid as needed to reach desired consistency. Season to taste with salt. Press **CANCEL**.

SERVE
Spoon potatoes into a serving bowl; if desired, sprinkle with chives and/or pepper.

*TIP: If cooking potatoes in water, add ½ teaspoon salt to the potatoes before cooking.

CHEESY GARLIC MASHED POTATOES: Prepare as above except add 4 cloves garlic, minced, to the potatoes before cooking and substitute 120ml soured cream, 40 g grated cheddar cheese and 25 g finely grated Parmesan cheese for the milk and butter.

SRIRACHA-RANCH MASHED POTATOES: Prepare as above except decrease milk to 60 ml and substitute 80ml bottled ranch dressing and 1 to 2 teaspoons bottled sriracha sauce for the butter.

Green Beans with Shallots & Pecans

While your turkey roasts in the oven, use the Instant Pot® to make this quick and delicious side dish.

PREP TIME	FUNCTION	CLOSED POT TIME	TOTAL TIME	RELEASE
15 minutes	Sauté (Normal); Steam	15 minutes	30 minutes + 5 minutes sauté	Quick

SERVES: 8

- 55 g pecan halves and pieces, coarsely chopped
- 240 ml water
- 675 g fresh green beans, stem ends trimmed
- 50 g unsalted butter
- 50 g finely chopped shallot
- 50 g packed brown sugar
- 1 teaspoon kosher salt
- ½ teaspoon coarsely ground black pepper

PREP

Select **SAUTÉ** on the Instant Pot® and adjust to **NORMAL**. Add the pecans and cook for 2 to 3 minutes or until lightly toasted, stirring often. Remove from the pot and set aside. Press **CANCEL**.

Fill a large bowl with water and ice; set aside. Add the 240 ml water and a vegetable steamer basket with legs to the pot.* Add the green beans to the steamer basket. Secure the lid on the pot. Close the pressure-release valve.

COOK

Select **STEAM** and adjust to 2 minutes. When cooking is complete, use a quick release to depressurise. Press **CANCEL**.

Carefully remove the steamer basket and transfer the beans to the ice water for 1 minute to stop the cooking. Transfer the beans to kitchen paper to dry. (Make sure the beans are dry before adding them to the pot in the next step.)

Thoroughly dry the inner pot. Select **SAUTÉ** and adjust to **NORMAL**. Add the butter to the pot. When butter is hot, add the shallot and cook for 2 to 3 minutes or until golden. Add the sugar, stirring constantly, until dissolved. Add the pecans and cook for 1 minute, stirring constantly. Add the green beans, salt and pepper, tossing to coat. Press **CANCEL**.

SERVE

Cook for 2 to 3 minutes or until the beans are heated through, tossing occasionally.

***TIP:** If your steamer basket doesn't have legs, place the trivet in the pot first, then place steamer basket on top of it.

Garlic Broccoli with Lemon & Olives

Steaming broccoli helps retain nutrients and its beautiful bright green colour. Its pleasing, cabbagey flavour is just right accented with lemon, garlic and olives.

PREP TIME	FUNCTION	CLOSED POT TIME	TOTAL TIME	RELEASE
10 minutes	Steam; Sauté (Normal)	10 minutes	20 minutes + 5 minutes sauté	Quick

SERVES: 4

- 240 ml water
- 700 g broccoli florets
- 1 tablespoon olive oil
- 3 cloves garlic, minced
- 40 g sliced Kalamata olives
- 2 teaspoons lemon zest
- 1 tablespoon fresh lemon juice
- ¼ teaspoon kosher salt
- ¼ teaspoon coarsely ground black pepper

PREP
Pour the water in the Instant Pot®. Place a steamer with legs in the pot.*
Add the broccoli to the steamer basket. Secure the lid on the pot. Close the pressure-release valve.

COOK
Select **STEAM** and adjust to 2 minutes. When cooking is complete, use a quick release to depressurise. Press **CANCEL**.

Carefully remove the steamer basket and transfer the broccoli to a bowl.

Thoroughly dry the inner pot. Select **SAUTÉ** and adjust to **NORMAL**. Add the oil. When the oil is hot, add the garlic, olives, lemon zest and juice and broccoli to the pot. Toss to combine. Cook and stir for 2 to 3 minutes or until the broccoli is heated through, tossing occasionally. Press **CANCEL**.

SERVE
Season the broccoli with salt and pepper.

*****TIP:** If your steamer basket doesn't have legs, place the trivet in the pot first, then place steamer basket on top of it.

Corn on the Cob with Herb Butter

Swap out the chives and flat-leaf parsley with different herbs if you like. Any soft-leaf herb such as basil, oregano, marjoram, tarragon or dill will do.

PREP TIME	FUNCTION		CLOSED POT TIME	TOTAL TIME	RELEASE
10 minutes	Steam (Less)		15 minutes	25 minutes	Quick

SERVES: 4

240 ml water

4 corns on the cob, kernels removed

50 g butter, softened

2 teaspoons chopped fresh chives

2 teaspoons chopped fresh flat-leaf parsley

⅛ teaspoon salt

Dash cayenne pepper

PREP
Place the trivet in the Instant Pot®. Add the water to the pot and place corn on the trivet. Secure the lid on the pot. Close the pressure-release valve.

COOK
Select **STEAM** and adjust to **LESS**. When cooking is complete, use a quick release to depressurise.

SERVE
While corn is steaming, for herb butter, combine butter, chives, parsley, salt and cayenne; mix well. Serve corn with herb butter.

Spring Greens with Smoked Ham Hocks & Sweet Onions

Collards can be quickly sautéed so they stay slightly firm or slow-simmered until they're very soft. Here, they're cooked to a perfect in-between stage and classically flavoured with smoked ham and sweet onions.

PREP TIME	FUNCTION	CLOSED POT TIME	TOTAL TIME	RELEASE
30 minutes	Sauté (Normal); Steam	15 minutes	45 minutes	Quick

SERVES: 6 to 8

- 6 slices smoked bacon, chopped
- 225 g smoked ham, diced
- 2 large sweet onions, peeled, quartered and thinly sliced (450 g)
- 80 ml apple cider vinegar
- 1 tablespoon brown sugar
- 1 teaspoon salt
- ¼ teaspoon black pepper
- 1 teaspoon hot pepper sauce
- 900 g to 1.1 kg fresh spring greens, washed, dried and coarsely chopped

PREP

Select **SAUTÉ** on the Instant Pot® and adjust to **NORMAL**. Add chopped bacon to pot. Cook and stir bacon for 5 to 10 minutes or until crisp. Using a slotted spoon, transfer crisp bacon to kitchen paper-lined plate to drain.

Add ham and onions to the pot; cook and stir for 5 to 6 minutes or until onions are limp and ham is browned. Press **CANCEL**; cool slightly. Add vinegar, sugar, salt, pepper and hot pepper sauce; mix well. Select **SAUTÉ** and adjust to **NORMAL**. Push spring greens into pot a batch at a time, waiting until one batch wilts down before adding another. Press **CANCEL**. When all greens are in the pot, secure the lid on the pot. Close the pressure-release valve.

COOK

Select **STEAM** and adjust cook time to 8 minutes. Once cooking is complete, use a quick release to depressurise.

SERVE

Using a slotted spoon, transfer greens to a serving dish; sprinkle with reserved crisp bacon bits.

Steamed Cauliflower with Cayenne & Parmesan

Just a few simple ingredients give this vegetable side wonderful flavour. Try it with a grilled steak.

PREP TIME	FUNCTION		CLOSED POT TIME	TOTAL TIME	RELEASE
10 minutes	Steam		15 minutes	25 minutes	Quick

SERVES: 4

240 ml water

2 kg large cauliflower florets

2 tablespoons butter, melted

1 tablespoon fresh lemon juice

¼ teaspoon salt

Dash cayenne pepper

35 g finely grated Parmesan cheese

1 tablespoon chopped fresh flat-leaf parsley

PREP
Place a vegetable steamer basket with legs in the Instant Pot®.* Add the water to pot and place cauliflower in basket. Secure the lid on pot. Close the pressure-release valve.

COOK
Select **STEAM** and adjust cook time to 1 minute. When cooking is complete, use a quick release to depressurise.

SERVE
Meanwhile, in a medium bowl combine butter, lemon juice, salt and cayenne. Add cooked cauliflower to butter mixture; stir gently to coat. Top with Parmesan and parsley.

*TIP: If your steamer basket doesn't have legs, place the trivet in the pot first, then place steamer basket on top of it.

Bacon-Basil Succotash

This Southern favourite gets gussied up with bacon, basil, jalapeño and garlic. It's just the thing to serve with a smoky ham steak.

PREP TIME	FUNCTION		CLOSED POT TIME	TOTAL TIME	RELEASE
25 minutes	Sauté (Normal); Steam		20 minutes	45 minutes	Quick

SERVES: 6 to 8

4	slices bacon, chopped
175	g coarsely chopped red pepper
75	g chopped red onion
1	jalapeño pepper, seeded and finely chopped
2	cloves garlic, minced
1	450-g packet frozen corn kernels
150	g frozen baby broad beans
120	ml chicken stock
20	g chopped fresh basil
	Salt and black pepper

PREP

Select **SAUTÉ** on the Instant Pot® and adjust to **NORMAL**. Add bacon to pot. Cook, stirring occasionally, until bacon is crisp for about 5 minutes. Transfer bacon to a bowl, leaving drippings in pot. Add pepper, onion, jalapeño and garlic to pot. Cook, stirring occasionally, until softened for about 3 minutes. Press **CANCEL**.

Stir in corn, broad beans and chicken stock. Secure the lid on the pot. Close the pressure-release valve.

COOK

Select **STEAM** and adjust cook time to 6 minutes. When cooking is complete, use a quick release to depressurise.

SERVE

Stir in the bacon and basil. Season to taste with salt and black pepper.

Brussels Sprouts with Bacon & Balsamic

After being steamed to tender perfection, the sprouts are browned with the bacon until they get a crisp, golden edge. A drizzle of balsamic vinegar adds a hint of sweetness.

PREP TIME	FUNCTION	CLOSED POT TIME	TOTAL TIME	RELEASE
20 minutes	Pressure/Manual (High); Sauté (Normal)	20 minutes	40 minutes	Quick

SERVES: 4

480 ml water

350 g fresh Brussels sprouts, trimmed and halved

5 slices bacon, chopped

2 tablespoons chopped fresh chives

2 tablespoons balsamic vinegar

¼ teaspoon black pepper

⅛ teaspoon salt

PREP

Place a vegetable steamer basket with legs in the Instant Pot®.* Add the water to the pot. Add Brussels sprouts to pot, arranging evenly in the steamer basket. Secure the lid on the pot. Close the pressure-release valve.

COOK

Select **MANUAL** and cook at high pressure for 2 minutes. When cooking is complete, use a quick release to depressurise. Press **CANCEL**. Transfer Brussels sprouts to a medium bowl. Remove steamer basket from pot; pour water from the pot. Wipe pot dry.

Select **SAUTÉ** and adjust to **NORMAL**. Add half of the Brussels sprouts and half of the bacon to the pot. Cook for 5 to 7 minutes or until sprouts are browned and bacon is crisp, stirring occasionally. Transfer sprouts and bacon to a serving dish; cover to keep warm. Repeat with remaining sprouts and bacon. Add to serving dish with first half of sprouts and bacon. Press **CANCEL**.

SERVE

Sprinkle sprouts with chives and drizzle with vinegar; sprinkle with pepper and salt. Toss quickly to coat. Serve immediately.

*__TIP:__ If your steamer basket doesn't have legs, place the trivet in the pot first, then place steamer basket on top of it.

Spicy Indian Savoy Cabbage

Deep green, crinkly-leaved Savoy cabbage has a mild, earthy flavour that takes beautifully to the Indian spices. The flavour of this dish is so complex and delicious you'll be tempted to eat it as your main course!

PREP TIME	FUNCTION	CLOSED POT TIME	TOTAL TIME	RELEASE
20 minutes	Sauté (Normal); Pressure/Manual (High)	5 minutes	25 minutes	Quick

SERVES: 4 to 6

- 1   5-cm piece fresh ginger, peeled and cut into 1-cm slices
- 4   cloves garlic, chopped
- 1   large jalapeño pepper, stemmed, halved and seeded
- 2   teaspoons garam masala
- 1   teaspoon ground turmeric
- 120   ml chicken stock
- 3   tablespoons coconut oil
- 1   tablespoon black mustard seeds
- 1   teaspoon coriander seeds
- 1   teaspoon cumin seeds
- 1   8-cm cinnamon stick
- 1   whole jalapeño pepper
- 300   g thinly sliced onions
- ½   teaspoon salt
- 675   g thinly sliced, cored Savoy cabbage
- 25   g snipped fresh coriander

PREP

In a food processor combine ginger, garlic, jalapeño, garam masala, turmeric and 60 ml of the stock. Cover and process until a coarse paste forms; set aside.

Select **SAUTÉ** on the Instant Pot® and adjust to **NORMAL**. Add the oil. When hot, add the mustard seeds, coriander seeds, cumin seeds, cinnamon stick and whole jalapeño. Cook, stirring frequently, for 2 minutes. (The mustard seeds will pop and spatter as they cook.) Add onions and cook for 4 to 5 minutes or until lightly browned. Add the ginger mixture and salt. Cook for 3 minutes, stirring often. Add the cabbage and remaining stock. Stir to combine from the bottom up. Press **CANCEL**.

Secure the lid on the pot. Close the pressure-release valve.

COOK

Select **MANUAL** and cook at high pressure for 3 minutes. When cooking is complete, use a quick release to depressurise.

SERVE

Remove and discard the cinnamon stick and whole jalapeño.

Sprinkle with coriander.

Maple-Vinegar-Braised Parsnips

Balsamic vinegar adds tanginess and maple syrup a bit of sweetness to this simple root-vegetable dish. Be sure to use real maple syrup for the best flavour.

PREP TIME	FUNCTION	CLOSED POT TIME	TOTAL TIME	RELEASE
15 minutes	Pressure/Manual (High)	10 minutes	25 minutes	Quick

SERVES: 4

- 675 g parsnips, peeled and cut into 1-cm slices on the diagonal
- 60 ml vegetable stock
- 3 tablespoons balsamic vinegar
- 2 tablespoons maple syrup
- Salt and black pepper

PREP
Combine the parsnips, stock and vinegar in the Instant Pot®.

Secure the lid on the pot. Close the pressure-release valve.

COOK
Select **MANUAL** and cook at high pressure for 4 minutes. When cooking is complete, use a quick release to depressurise.

Stir in the maple syrup. Season to taste with salt and pepper.

SERVE
Transfer to a bowl and serve.

Jill Nussinow blogs at TheVeggieQueen.com and is the author of *Vegan Under Pressure*.

Mashed Sweet Potatoes with Streusel Topping

We love this trick: The streusel topping is browned on Sauté in the Instant Pot® before being removed and set aside to cool, so it stays crunchy even after it's sprinkled on the cooked sweet potatoes right before serving.

PREP TIME	FUNCTION	CLOSED POT TIME	TOTAL TIME
20 minutes	Sauté (Normal); Slow Cook (More)	3 hours 30 minutes	3 hours 50 minutes

SERVES: 8

STREUSEL TOPPING

1 tablespoon butter

25 g rolled oats

2 tablespoons coconut flakes

2 tablespoons chopped pecans

2 tablespoons brown sugar

Dash cinnamon

SWEET POTATOES

900 g sweet potatoes, peeled and cut into 5-cm chunks

175 ml orange juice

Zest of 1 orange (1 tablespoon)

PREP

For the streusel topping, select **SAUTÉ** on Instant Pot® and adjust to **NORMAL**. When hot, add the butter to the pot. When melted, add the oats, coconut and pecans. Cook for about 5 minutes until lightly toasted, stirring frequently. Stir in brown sugar and cinnamon. Press **CANCEL**. Pour onto a plate to cool.

Add sweet potatoes to the pot. Pour orange juice over the sweet potatoes and toss so that all sides of the potatoes have been coated with orange juice. Secure the lid on the pot. Open the pressure-release valve.

COOK

Select **SLOW COOK** and adjust to **MORE**. Cook for 3½ hours until potatoes are very tender.

SERVE

Add orange zest to undrained potatoes and mash until smooth. Transfer to a serving bowl. Sprinkle with streusel topping.

Orange-Honey Beetroots with Parsley

Beetroots are one of the best vegetables to cook in the Instant Pot®. Their dense texture usually requires a long cook time, but they cook quickly under pressure – and they turn out fork-tender, never mushy.

PREP TIME	FUNCTION	CLOSED POT TIME	TOTAL TIME	RELEASE
25 minutes	Manual/Pressure (High)	35 minutes	1 hour	Natural

SERVES: 4

- 2 tablespoons olive oil
- 2 shallots, chopped
- 1.3 kg beetroots (with tops), trimmed, peeled and cut into 5-cm chunks
- 120 ml freshly squeezed orange juice
- 3 tablespoons red wine vinegar
- 3 tablespoons honey
- ½ teaspoon salt
- ½ teaspoon black pepper
- 1 tablespoon chopped fresh flat-leaf parsley
- 1 teaspoon orange zest

PREP
Select **SAUTÉ** on the Instant Pot® and adjust to **NORMAL**. Add olive oil and shallots. Cook, stirring often, until shallots are softened for about 3 minutes. Press **CANCEL**. Stir in the beetroots, orange juice, vinegar, honey, salt and pepper. Secure the lid on the pot. Close the pressure-release valve.

COOK
Select **MANUAL** and cook at high pressure for 13 minutes. When cooking is complete, use a natural release to depressurise.

SERVE
Stir in parsley and orange zest.

Artichoke 'Nests' with Garlic Clove Eggs

As pretty to look at as they are delicious to eat, these make a fitting first course for a fancy dinner party in the spring, when artichokes are in season. Your guests will be so impressed!

PREP TIME	FUNCTION	CLOSED POT TIME	TOTAL TIME	RELEASE
35 minutes	Steam; Sauté (Normal)	20 minutes	55 minutes	Quick

SERVES: 4

- 120 ml olive oil
- 60 ml freshly squeezed lemon juice
- 1 teaspoon honey
- 570 ml chicken stock
- 2 medium artichokes (about 225 g each)
- 12 whole cloves garlic, peeled
- 1 tablespoon snipped fresh dill
- 1 teaspoon salt
- ½ teaspoon black pepper
- 1 bay leaf

PREP

Combine the oil, lemon juice, honey and chicken stock in the Instant Pot®. Mix well.

Use kitchen shears to snip the thorny tips of each of the leaves on the artichokes. Cut artichokes in half lengthwise. Using a serrated spoon or paring knife, carefully remove the artichokes' thorny centres. Place artichokes in the pot, turning each to coat with liquid. Turn artichokes so cut sides are above oil mixture, packed tightly together. Place 3 garlic cloves in the indentation of each artichoke half. Sprinkle artichokes with dill, salt and pepper. Drop bay leaf into pot. Secure the lid on the pot. Close the pressure-release valve.

COOK

Select **STEAM** and adjust cook time to 9 minutes. When cooking is complete, use a quick release to depressurise. Press **CANCEL**.

Using a slotted spoon, remove artichokes and transfer to serving plates.

Select **SAUTÉ** and adjust to **NORMAL**. Let liquid boil for 5 minutes or until slightly reduced. Remove and discard bay leaf. Skim fat from top of liquid. Press **CANCEL**.

SERVE

Spoon liquid over artichokes. Serve warm or at room temperature.

Soups, Stews & Chilli

Beef Burgundy

Chuck steak – a tough cut of meat – gets butter-knife-tender after slow cooking in a blend of dry red wine and beef stock flavoured with bacon, baby onions and herbs. Look for fines herbes in the spice aisle of your supermarket. The classic blend is chervil, chives, parsley and tarragon.

PREP TIME	FUNCTION	CLOSED POT TIME	TOTAL TIME
35 minutes	Sauté (Normal); Slow Cook (More)	4 hours	4 hours 35 minutes

SERVES: 6

- 30 g plain flour
- ½ teaspoon salt
- ¼ teaspoon black pepper
- 4 slices bacon, chopped
- 2 tablespoons butter
- 900 g beef chuck steak, trimmed of excess fat and cut into 2.5-cm cubes
- 400 g bag frozen baby onions, thawed
- 225 g button mushrooms, cleaned and cut in half
- 1 teaspoon fines herbes
- 240 ml burgundy wine or dry red wine blend
- 360 ml beef stock
- 225 g egg noodles, cooked according to packet instructions
- 1½ teaspoons chopped fresh flat-leaf parsley

PREP

Combine flour, salt and pepper in a resealable plastic bag. Close bag; shake to mix well. Set aside.

Add bacon to the Instant Pot®. Select **SAUTÉ** on the Instant Pot® and adjust to **NORMAL**. Cook and stir bacon for 5 to 7 minutes or until crisp. Remove crisp bacon with a slotted spoon; transfer to kitchen paper to drain. Chill until serving time.

Press **CANCEL**. Carefully remove inner pot; pour bacon fat into another container. Replace pot. Add butter; select **SAUTÉ** and adjust to **NORMAL**. Add beef cubes to flour mixture in bag. Shake to coat cubes with flour. Brown beef cubes, half at a time, in butter on all sides. Transfer to a bowl. Add onions to pot. Cook and stir for 1 minute. Add onions to reserved beef cubes.

Add mushrooms to pot, adding more butter if necessary. Cook and stir until golden. Press **CANCEL**. Return reserved beef cubes, onions and fines herbes to the pot. Stir in wine and beef stock; mix gently. Secure the lid on the pot. Open the pressure-release valve.

COOK

Select **SLOW COOK** and adjust to **MORE**. Cook for 4 hours.

SERVE

When cooking is complete, spoon beef burgundy over hot cooked noodles. Sprinkle with parsley and reserved bacon.

Greek Beef Stifado

This classic stew is flavoured with aromatic spices – whole allspice and whole cloves. They infuse the dish with a warm, slightly sweet flavour – a lovely balance to the acidity of the tomatoes and red wine. They soften enough in the marinating and cooking time that you won't mind eating them whole.

PREP TIME	FUNCTION	CLOSED POT TIME	TOTAL TIME	RELEASE
1 hour	Sauté (Normal); Meat/Stew (Normal)	1 hour 5 minutes	2 hours 5 minutes + 6 hours marinate	Natural

SERVES: 8

- 1 1.3-kg to 1.6-kg beef chuck steak, cut into 2-cm cubes
- 4 cloves garlic, minced
- 2 bay leaves
- 15 whole allspice berries, bruised
- 10 whole cloves
- 1 teaspoon dried oregano
- 160 ml dry red wine
- 60 ml red wine vinegar
- 3 tablespoons olive oil
- 1 450-g packet frozen white baby onions, thawed and patted dry
- 4 large ripe tomatoes, peeled and chopped
- 55 g tomato purée
- Salt and black pepper
- 450 g orzo, cooked according to packet instructions
- 50 g shredded Pecorino cheese

PREP

Place cubed beef in a large non-metallic container. Add garlic, bay leaves, allspice, cloves, oregano, red wine and red wine vinegar. Mix well. Cover and chill for at least 6 hours or up to overnight.

Drain beef cubes, reserving marinade. Pour olive oil into Instant Pot®. Select **SAUTÉ** and adjust to **NORMAL**. Working in small batches, brown beef cubes in oil until browned on all sides. Transfer browned meat to a plate. Working in small batches, brown onions in oil. Transfer browned onions to a plate. Press **CANCEL**.

Return beef cubes, accumulated juices and onions to the pot. Add reserved marinade, tomatoes and tomato puree. Stir gently.

Secure the lid on the pot. Close the pressure-release valve.

COOK

Select **MEAT/STEW** and adjust to **NORMAL**. When cooking is complete, use a natural release to depressurise.

SERVE

Remove and discard bay leaves. Season with salt and pepper to taste. Serve stew over cooked orzo. Top with cheese.

Beef Chilli

While the chilli cooks in the Instant Pot®, bake a batch of corn bread in the oven. Everything will be ready at the same time.

PREP TIME	FUNCTION	CLOSED POT TIME	TOTAL TIME	RELEASE
20 minutes	Sauté (Normal); Pressure/Manual (High)	1 hour	1 hour 20 minutes	Natural

SERVES: 8

- 675 g minced beef
- 150 g chopped onion
- 4 cloves garlic, minced
- 1 425-g tin tomato sauce
- 2 425-g to 450-g tins kidney beans, drained
- 240 ml beef stock
- 2 400-g tins diced tomatoes, undrained
- 2 tablespoons chilli powder
- ½ teaspoon black pepper
- 1 125-g tin diced green chillis, undrained (optional)
- Hot sauce (optional)
- Grated cheddar cheese, soured cream and/or sliced spring onions

PREP
Select **SAUTÉ** on the Instant Pot® and adjust to **NORMAL**. Cook beef, onion and garlic for about 10 minutes or until the meat is browned and onion is tender. Press **CANCEL**. Add tomato sauce, beans, stock, tomatoes, chilli powder, black pepper and green chillis (if using). Secure the lid on the pot. Close the pressure-release valve.

COOK
Select **MANUAL** and cook at high pressure for 10 minutes. When cooking is complete, use a natural release to depressurise.

SERVE
Serve chilli with hot sauce (if using), cheese, soured cream and/or spring onions.

Pork Posole Rojo

Posole is a classic Mexican stew featuring meat and chewy hominy (dried and rehydrated corn) in a chilli-laced stock. Toppings such as radish, shredded cabbage, onion, coriander and avocado give it a fresh touch.

PREP TIME	FUNCTION	CLOSED POT TIME	TOTAL TIME	RELEASE
15 minutes	Sauté (More); Meat/Stew	1 hour 20 minutes	1 hour 35 minutes	Natural

SERVES: 6

- 2 tablespoons olive oil
- 900 g pork ribs
- 1 small onion, peeled and quartered
- 6 garlic cloves, peeled
- 2 tablespoons ancho chilli powder
- 480 ml water
- 1 teaspoon salt
- 950 ml chicken stock
- 1 teaspoon oregano
- 2 425-g tins white hominy, drained

OPTIONAL TOPPINGS

Thinly sliced radishes

Shredded cabbage

Coarsely chopped fresh coriander

Thinly sliced red onion

Cubed ripe avocado

Lime wedges for squeezing

PREP

Select **SAUTÉ** on the Instant Pot® and adjust to **MORE**. Add oil to pot. When oil is hot, brown ribs in batches until browned on all sides for about 5 minutes per batch. Add all ribs back to pot. Press **CANCEL**.

In a blender container combine onion, garlic, chilli powder, the water and salt. Blend until smooth. Add onion-chilli mixture to pot. Add chicken stock, oregano, hominy and pork ribs to pot. Secure the lid on the pot. Close the pressure-release valve.

COOK

Select **MEAT/STEW**. When cooking time is complete, use a natural release to depressurise.

SERVE

Remove ribs from the pot and coarsely shred meat. Return shredded meat to pot. Divide posole among serving bowls and top with desired toppings.

Neapolitan Pork-Pumpkin Stew

In most of Italy, pumpkin is a much-loved autumn vegetable savoured in fancy restaurants as well as in simple country fare like this stew.

PREP TIME	FUNCTION	CLOSED POT TIME	TOTAL TIME	RELEASE
45 minutes	Sauté (Normal/More); Pressure/Manual (High)	20 minutes	1 hour 5 minutes	Quick

SERVES: 6

- 6 slices bacon, chopped
- 450 g pork tenderloin, trimmed and cut into bite-size pieces
- 5 cloves garlic, minced
- 1.7 litres chicken stock
- 2 fennel bulbs, trimmed and coarsely chopped, fronds reserved
- 800 g 4-cm cubes of pumpkin* or butternut squash
- 100 g dry ditalini pasta, macaroni or mini penne
- ¼ teaspoon chilli flakes (optional)
- ¼ teaspoon salt
- ⅛ teaspoon black pepper

UPREP

Select **SAUTÉ** and adjust to **NORMAL**. Add bacon to pot. Cook and stir until bacon is crispy, about 6 to 8 minutes. Press **CANCEL**. Remove bacon to a kitchen paper-lined plate to drain. Remove all but about 1 tablespoon bacon fat from the pot.

Select **SAUTÉ** and adjust to **MORE**. Brown pork cubes, half at a time, on all sides in the drippings. As pork cubes brown, remove to a plate with a slotted spoon and set aside.

When all pork is browned, add garlic to the pot. Cook, stirring constantly, for 1 minute or until golden. Press **CANCEL**. Add 60ml of the chicken stock. Scrape bottom and sides of pot to loosen browned bits.

Add remaining chicken stock, fennel, pumpkin and pasta to pot. Stir in the reserved pork and accumulated juices, chilli flakes (if using), salt and black pepper. Secure the lid on the pot. Close the pressure-release valve.

COOK

Select **MANUAL** and cook at high pressure for 1 minute. When cooking is complete, use a quick release to depressurise (there may be some spattering out of the top of the pot).

SERVE

Let stew stand for 3 to 4 minutes before serving. Top with coarsely chopped fennel fronds and crisped bacon.

*TIP: Pumpkins for cooking are smaller than decorative pumpkins and have sweet, dense flesh. You'll find them in the vegetable section of the supermarket.

Dutch Brown-Bean Stew

This hearty stew of brown beans, sausage, onions, carrots, red-skin potatoes and apples has autumn written all over it. If you can't find brown beans, pinto beans make a perfectly fine substitute.

PREP TIME	FUNCTION	CLOSED POT TIME	TOTAL TIME	RELEASE
25 minutes	Sauté (Normal); Pressure/Manual (High)	1 hour 25 minutes	1 hour 50 minutes	Natural/Quick

SERVES: 6 to 8

- 225 g bacon, sliced crosswise into 0.5-cm strips
- 350 to 400g smoked sausage, cut into 1-cm rounds
- 200 g dried brown beans or pinto beans, picked over and rinsed
- 950 ml chicken stock
- 2 medium yellow onions, peeled, halved and sliced 0.5 cm thick
- 1 teaspoon salt
- 1 450-g bag baby carrots
- 2 medium Granny Smith apples, peeled, cored and cut into 8 wedges each
- 550 g B-size red-skin new potatoes, quartered
- Black pepper
- 1½ teaspoons finely chopped fresh flat-leaf parsley

PREP
Select **SAUTÉ** on the Instant Pot® and adjust to **NORMAL**. Add bacon and sausage to pot. Cook, stirring frequently, for 6 to 7 minutes or until bacon edges are brown and crisp. Press **CANCEL**. Using a small ladle or spoon, remove excess fat from the pot and discard. Add beans, stock, onions and salt to pot. Stir to combine.

Secure the lid on the pot. Close the pressure-release valve.

COOK
Select **MANUAL** and cook at high pressure for 30 minutes. When cooking is complete, use a natural release to depressurise. Press **CANCEL**.

Add carrots, apples and potatoes to pot. Secure the lid on the pot. Select **MANUAL** and cook at high pressure for 3 minutes. When cooking is complete, use a quick release to depressurise.

SERVE
Season to taste with black pepper. Ladle stew into bowls. Sprinkle with parsley.

Chicken Noodle Soup

This tastes just like the chicken noodle soup your grandmother made – with the addition of red sweet pepper and baby spinach.

PREP TIME	FUNCTION		CLOSED POT TIME	TOTAL TIME	RELEASE
15 minutes	Poultry (More); Pressure/Manual (High); Sauté (Normal)		2 hours	2 hours 15 minutes	Natural/Quick

SERVES: 8

- 1   1.6-kg to 1.8-kg whole chicken
- 1   large red onion
- 3   stalks celery
- 1   bay leaf
- 1.5   litres chicken stock
- 2   medium carrots, thinly sliced
- 1   medium red pepper, coarsely chopped
- 150   g dried wide egg noodles
- 4   cloves garlic, minced
- 1   teaspoon salt
- ½   teaspoon dried thyme
- ½   teaspoon sage
- ½   teaspoon black pepper
- 75   g fresh baby spinach leaves
    Juice of 1 lemon (3 to 4 tablespoons)

PREP

Place chicken in the Instant Pot®. Cut onion in half; set half aside. Cut remaining half into wedges; place on top of chicken. Cut 1 stalk of celery in half; add to pot with chicken. Add bay leaf to pot. Slowly pour stock over everything in the pot.

COOK

Secure the lid on the pot. Close the pressure-release valve. Select **POULTRY** and adjust to **MORE**. When cooking is complete, use a natural release to depressurise. Press **CANCEL**.

Meanwhile, chop reserved red onion half. Thinly slice remaining 2 stalks celery. Set aside. Once pressure is released from the pot, transfer the chicken to a large cutting board; set aside. Use a slotted spoon to remove and discard onion wedges, celery stalk and bay leaf from liquid in pot. If desired, strain liquid in pot through a fine-mesh sieve; return liquid to pot if strained. Skim fat from top of liquid in pot if desired.

Add chopped onion, sliced celery, carrots, pepper, noodles, garlic, salt, thyme, sage and black pepper to pot. Secure the lid on the pot. Close the pressure-release valve.

Select **MANUAL** and cook at high pressure for 2 minutes. When cooking is complete, use a quick release to depressurise. Press **CANCEL**.

SERVE

When chicken is cool enough to handle, remove meat from bones. Discard bones and skin. Cut meat into bite-size pieces. Add chicken to soup in the pot. Select **SAUTÉ** and adjust to **NORMAL**. Cook, uncovered, for 1 to 2 minutes or until soup is heated through. Press **CANCEL**. Stir in spinach and lemon juice just before serving.

ASIAN-STYLE CHICKEN NOODLE SOUP: Prepare as directed except substitute 225 g rice noodles for the egg noodles, substitute 2 tablespoons reduced-salt soy sauce for the salt, substitute 3 to 4 tablespoons rice vinegar for the lemon juice, substitute shredded Chinese cabbage for the spinach and substitute 2 tablespoons finely chopped fresh ginger for the dried thyme.

Chicken Pho

Pho (fuh) has taken the country by storm – and it's no wonder. This Vietnamese version of chicken noodle soup features chicken and rice noodles in an aromatic stock that is topped with bean sprouts and fresh herbs.

PREP TIME	FUNCTION	CLOSED POT TIME	TOTAL TIME
35 minutes	Sauté (Normal); Slow Cook (More)	4 hours	4 hours 35 minutes

SERVES: 4 to 6

- 1 tablespoon vegetable oil
- 6 bone-in chicken thighs, skinned
- ½ teaspoon salt
- ¼ teaspoon black pepper
- 2 large shallots, finely chopped
- ½ teaspoon sugar
- 225 g shiitake mushrooms, stemmed and sliced
- 950 ml chicken stock
- 450 ml water
- 2 teaspoons fish sauce
- 1 5-cm piece fresh ginger, thinly sliced
- 1 cinnamon stick, broken in half
- 3 whole cloves
- 1 star anise
- 1 225-g to 350-g packet rice noodles, cooked according to packet instructions
- 1 bunch coriander, chopped
- 1 bunch Thai basil or sweet basil, chopped
- 200 g bean sprouts
- 50 g sliced spring onions
- 2 jalapeño peppers, sliced
- 1 lime, cut into small wedges
  Hoisin sauce (optional)

PREP

Select **SAUTÉ** and adjust to **NORMAL**. Add oil to pot. Season chicken with salt and black pepper. When oil is hot, add half of the chicken to pot. Cook chicken until browned, turning once, for about 12 minutes. Remove chicken from pot. Repeat with remaining chicken. Add shallots and sugar. Cook and stir until shallots are softened and lightly browned for about 3 minutes. Add mushrooms; cook and stir for 2 minutes more. Press **CANCEL**. Add chicken stock, the water and fish sauce. Return all chicken to pot.

Prepare spice bag: Place ginger, cinnamon stick, cloves and star anise on a double-thick, 15-cm square of 100%-cotton cheesecloth. Bring up corners and tie closed with 100%-cotton string. Add to pot. Secure the lid on the pot. Open the pressure-release valve.

COOK

Select **SLOW COOK** and adjust to **MORE**. Cook for 4 to 4½ hours or until chicken is tender. Press **CANCEL**.

SERVE

Carefully remove chicken and spice bag from pot. Discard spice bag. When chicken is cool enough to handle, remove the meat; return meat to pot. Discard bones.

Serve soup in large bowls. Add desired amount of rice noodles to each bowl. Top with coriander, basil, bean sprouts, spring onions and jalapeños as desired. Serve with lime wedges and hoisin sauce (if using).

Chicken & Shrimp Gumbo

Okra is a traditional component of gumbo, not only because it was a vegetable familiar to the African-American cooks who created the dish but also because it has a natural thickening agent.

PREP TIME	FUNCTION	CLOSED POT TIME	TOTAL TIME	RELEASE
45 minutes	Sauté (Normal); Pressure/Manual (High)	35 minutes	1 hour 20 minutes	Quick

SERVES: 8

- 1 tablespoon vegetable oil
- 450 g skinless, boneless chicken thighs, cut into 5-cm pieces
- 60 ml vegetable oil
- 60 g plain flour
- 1 tablespoon Cajun seasoning
- 1 tablespoon dried thyme
- 1 teaspoon smoked paprika
- ½ teaspoon kosher salt
- 150 g chopped onion
- 175 g chopped green pepper
- 2 stalks celery, chopped
- 4 cloves garlic, minced
- 950 ml chicken stock
- 1 400-g tin diced tomatoes, undrained
- 450 g medium prawns, peeled and deveined
- 200 g frozen sliced okra
- 1 kg to 1.2 kg hot cooked rice
- Chopped fresh flat-leaf parsley

PREP

Select **SAUTÉ** on the Instant Pot® and adjust to **NORMAL**. Add the 1 tablespoon oil to the pot. When hot, add the chicken. Cook for 5 to 6 minutes or until browned. Using a slotted spoon, transfer the chicken to a bowl, leaving any fat in the pot.

Add the 60 ml oil, flour, Cajun seasoning, thyme, paprika and salt to the pot. Cook, stirring constantly, for 5 minutes. Add the onion, pepper, celery and garlic to the pot. Cook, stirring constantly, for 3 to 5 minutes or until the vegetables are softened. Press **CANCEL**. Add the chicken and any juices in the bowl, stock and tomatoes to the pot. Secure the lid on the pot. Close the pressure-release valve.

COOK

Select **MANUAL** and cook at high pressure for 10 minutes. When cooking is complete, use a quick release to depressurise. Press **CANCEL**.

Select **SAUTÉ** and adjust to **NORMAL**. Add the prawns and okra to the pot and cook for 5 minutes or until okra is crisp-tender and prawns are cooked through. Press **CANCEL**.

SERVE

Ladle the gumbo over the hot cooked rice and sprinkle with parsley.

Chicken & Wild Rice Soup

This soup gets its richness from a combination of whipping cream and cream cheese. The sherry cuts through the richness and adds a depth of flavour but isn't a necessity.

PREP TIME	FUNCTION	CLOSED POT TIME	TOTAL TIME	RELEASE
30 minutes	Pressure/Manual (High); Sauté (Normal)	1 hour 35 minutes	2 hours 5 minutes	Natural

SERVES: 6

- 900 g bone-in chicken breast halves, skinned
- 170 g dried wild rice, rinsed and drained
- 1.25 litres reduced-salt chicken stock
- 2 medium carrots, thinly sliced
- 75 g sliced fresh button mushrooms
- 1 stalk celery, thinly sliced
- 75 g chopped onion
- 55 g dry long grain white rice
- 3 cloves garlic, minced
- 1 teaspoon dried thyme
- 180 ml whipping cream or single cream
- 115 g cream cheese, softened and cut into cubes
- 60 ml dry sherry (optional)
- 10 g chopped fresh flat-leaf parsley

PREP
Place chicken and wild rice in the Instant Pot®. Pour stock over everything. Secure the lid on the pot. Close the pressure-release valve.

COOK
Select **MANUAL** and cook at high pressure for 10 minutes. When cooking is complete, use a natural release to depressurise. Press **CANCEL**.

Transfer chicken to a cutting board; set aside. Add carrots, mushrooms, celery, onion, white rice, garlic and thyme to rice mixture in pot.

Secure the lid on the pot. Close the pressure-release valve. Select **MANUAL** and cook at high pressure for 5 minutes. When cooking is complete, use a natural release to depressurise. Press **CANCEL**.

Meanwhile, remove chicken from bones; discard bones. Cut chicken into bite-size pieces. Add chicken, whipping cream, cream cheese and sherry (if using) to the pot. Select **SAUTÉ** and adjust to **NORMAL**. Cook and stir for 1 to 2 minutes or until heated through and cream cheese is completely melted and smooth. Press **CANCEL**.

SERVE
Ladle soup into bowls. Sprinkle with parsley.

Brazilian Black-Bean Soup

This filling and nutritious soup is considered the national dish of Brazil. To make your own *feijoada* (fay-SHWA-da) truly tango, serve it over hot cooked rice with stewed collards on the side.

PREP TIME	FUNCTION		CLOSED POT TIME	TOTAL TIME	RELEASE
25 minutes	Pressure/Manual (High)		1 hour 5 minutes	1 hour 30 minutes	Natural

SERVES: 6

- 225 g chopped onions
- 50 g thinly sliced spring onions
- 2 cloves garlic
- 350 g dried black beans
- 1 smoked pork hock
- 2 bay leaves
- 2 teaspoons ground coriander
- Stems of 1 bunch coriander, tied with kitchen string
- 2 teaspoons finely shredded orange zest
- Juice of 1 large orange
- 360 ml chicken stock
- Hot cooked rice (optional)
- 2 oranges, peeled and sectioned*
- 25 g chopped fresh coriander or flat-leaf parsley

PREP

Combine onions, spring onions, garlic, black beans, pork hock, bay leaves, coriander, coriander stems, orange zest, orange juice and chicken stock in the Instant Pot®. Secure the lid on the pot. Close the pressure-release valve.

COOK

Select **MANUAL** and cook on high pressure for 40 minutes. When cooking is complete, use a natural release to depressurise.

SERVE

Remove coriander stems and bay leaves and discard. Remove pork hock and transfer to a cutting board. Using two forks, shred meat and return to pot; mix well.

Serve as a soup or, if desired, over cooked white rice. Garnish with orange sections; sprinkle with chopped coriander.

*TIP: To section an orange, cut a thin slice off of the stem end and bottom of the orange to expose the fruit. Stand the fruit upright on a cutting board. Cut sections of peel off the orange from top to bottom, following the curve of the fruit. To release the sections, insert a small thin knife on either side of each one, cutting from the outside of the fruit toward the centre.

Black Bean & Mushroom Chilli

With cumin, oregano and a double dose of smoke from both smoked paprika and chipotle powder, this flavourful vegan chilli doesn't need added salt.

PREP TIME	FUNCTION		CLOSED POT TIME	TOTAL TIME	RELEASE
20 minutes	Pressure/Manual (High)		20 minutes	40 minutes	Quick

SERVES: 8

- 450 g chopped onion
- 8 cloves garlic, minced
- 900 g mushrooms, sliced
- 2 400-g tins salt-free diced tomatoes, undrained
- 3 425-g tins salt-free black beans, undrained
- 1 tablespoon cumin
- 1 tablespoon oregano
- ½ tablespoon smoked paprika
- ½ teaspoon chipotle powder
- 450 g frozen corn, defrosted
- Baked potato or cooked brown rice (optional)
- Parmesan

PREP

Combine onions, garlic, mushrooms, tomatoes, black beans, cumin, oregano, smoked paprika and chipotle powder in the Instant Pot®. Secure the lid on the pot. Close the pressure-release valve.

COOK

Select **MANUAL** and cook at high pressure for 6 minutes. When cooking is complete, use a quick release to depressurise. Stir in the corn.

SERVE

Sprinkle with Parmesan. If desired, serve over a baked potato or brown rice.

ENLIGHTENED FAUX PARMESAN: In a food processor or blender combine 100 g rolled oats, 40 g nutritional yeast and 1 tablespoon salt-free seasoning. Blend until powdery.

TIP: If desired, use the **SAUTÉ** function and sauté the onion, garlic and mushrooms first.

Chef AJ blogs at EatUnprocessed.com.

Indian-Style Lentil Soup

Some brands of garam masala contain salt. If the brand you are using doesn't contain salt, you may need to add this to taste to the finished soup. Toasting the spice blend briefly intensifies its flavour.

PREP TIME	FUNCTION	CLOSED POT TIME	TOTAL TIME
20 minutes	Sauté (Normal); Slow Cook (More)	3 hours 30 minutes	3 hours 50 minutes

SERVES: 6

- 1 **tablespoon butter**
- 1 **medium onion, chopped**
- 3 **cloves garlic, finely chopped**
- 1 **tablespoon chopped fresh ginger**
- 1 **jalapeño pepper, seeded and finely chopped**
- 2 **teaspoons garam masala**
- 450 **g dried lentils, rinsed**
- 2 **litres vegetable or chicken stock**
- 1 **tablespoon fresh lemon juice**
  Plain yogurt (optional)
  Chopped fresh coriander (optional)

PREP

Select **SAUTÉ** on the Instant Pot® and adjust to **NORMAL**. When hot, add butter to pot. Add onion, garlic, ginger and jalapeño. Cook for 1 minute. Add garam masala and cook for an additional 1 minute. Add lentils and stock. Stir to combine. Press **CANCEL**. Secure the lid on the pot. Open the pressure-release valve.

COOK

Select **SLOW COOK** and adjust to **MORE**. Cook for 3½ to 4½ hours until lentils are very tender.

SERVE

Add lemon juice to pot. (Soup can be served as is or, for a creamier version, use an immersion blender for 30 seconds to puree some of the lentils.)

Ladle into soup bowls. If desired, garnish with plain yogurt and coriander.

Italian White-Bean Soup

If you can find escarole, a broad-leaved endive lettuce, give it a try. Popular in Italian cooking, it can be enjoyed raw as a salad green and cooked as a vegetable.

PREP TIME	FUNCTION	CLOSED POT TIME	TOTAL TIME	RELEASE
10 minutes	Sauté (Normal); Soup/Stock	1 hour 10 minutes	1 hour 20 minutes	Natural

SERVES: 4 to 6

1½ tablespoons olive oil

2 tablespoons sliced garlic

¼ teaspoon chilli flakes

200 g dried unsoaked or cannellini beans, rinsed and drained

1 bay leaf

1.5 litres reduced-salt chicken stock

600 g coarsely chopped kale or escarole

35 g grated Parmigiano-Reggiano or Grana Padano cheese

Toasted Italian bread (optional)

PREP

Select **SAUTÉ** on the Instant Pot® and adjust to **NORMAL**. When hot, add olive oil, garlic and chilli flakes. Sauté for 1 minute. Press **CANCEL**. Add beans, bay leaf and stock. Secure the lid on the pot. Close the pressure-release valve.

COOK

Select **SOUP/STOCK**. When cooking is complete, use a natural release to depressurise.

SERVE

If desired, use a potato masher to mash some of the beans for a thicker consistency. Stir in kale and cheese. Divide soup among bowls. If desired, serve with toasted Italian bread.

Vegan Barlotti Bean, Millet & Bulgur Chilli

Millet is the crunchy round yellow grain with a cornlike flavour that is often an element in hearty artisan-style wholegrain breads. Here it adds texture and interest to a vegan chilli.

PREP TIME	FUNCTION	CLOSED POT TIME	TOTAL TIME	RELEASE
10 minutes	Pressure/Manual (High)	1 hour	1 hour 10 minutes	Natural

SERVES: 6 to 8

450 g dried Barlotti beans, pinto beans or black beans

125 ml water

1 400-g tin diced tomatoes with green chillis

85 g bulgur or quinoa

50 g millet

2 tablespoons tomato paste

1½ teaspoons ground cumin

1 teaspoon chilli powder

1 teaspoon minced garlic

1 teaspoon dried oregano

½ teaspoon liquid smoke (optional)

½ teaspoon chipotle powder

Salt and black pepper

Optional toppings: Cashew cream, vegan grated cheese, hot sauce, pickled jalapeño peppers

PREP
Combine the beans and 710 ml of the water in the Instant Pot®. Secure the lid on the pot. Close the pressure-release valve.

COOK
Select **MANUAL** and cook at high pressure for 25 minutes. When cooking is complete, use a natural release to depressurise.

Add the remaining 480 ml water, the tomatoes, bulgur, millet, tomato paste, cumin, chilli powder, garlic, oregano, liquid smoke (if using) and the chipotle powder.

Secure the lid on the pot. Close the pressure-release valve. Select **MANUAL** and cook at high pressure for 10 minutes. When cooking is complete, use a natural release to depressurise.

SERVE
Season with salt and black pepper to taste. If desired, serve with optional toppings.

Kathy Hester is the creator of HealthySlowCooking.com and author of The *Ultimate Vegan Cookbook for Your Instant Pot®.*

Spicy Brown Rice & Bean Soup

Adding the vegetables to the hot soup after the beans are cooked in the stock preserves their crisp-tender texture and nutritional content.

PREP TIME	FUNCTION	CLOSED POT TIME	TOTAL TIME	RELEASE
20 minutes	Sauté (Normal); Pressure/Manual (High)	1 hour	1 hour 20 minutes + 5 minutes	Natural

SERVES: 4 to 6

- 1 tablespoon olive oil
- 150 g diced onion
- 4 cloves garlic, minced
- 1 jalapeño pepper, seeded and minced (optional)
- 1 tablespoon ground cumin
- 1 tablespoon paprika
- 1 bay leaf
- 170 g brown rice
- 150 g unsoaked dried pinto beans, rinsed and drained
- 150 g unsoaked dried black beans, rinsed and drained
- 1.5 litres vegetable stock
- 150 g to 300 g chopped summer squash, broccoli, green beans, corn or any greens
- 3 tablespoons fresh lime juice (about 2 limes)
- 2 tablespoons snipped fresh coriander
- Salt and black pepper

PREP

Select **SAUTÉ** on the Instant Pot® and adjust to **NORMAL**. When hot, add the oil. Add the onion and cook, stirring occasionally, for 2 minutes. Add the garlic, chilli (if using), cumin and paprika. Cook for 1 minute. Add the bay leaf, rice, beans and stock. Press **CANCEL**.

Secure the lid on the pot. Close the pressure-release valve.

COOK

Select **MANUAL** and cook at high pressure for 30 minutes. When cooking is complete, use a natural release to depressurise.

SERVE

Remove and discard the bay leaf. Add the summer squash or other vegetables. Cover the pot with the lid. Let stand for 5 minutes.

Add the lime juice and coriander. Season to taste with salt and black pepper.

 Jill Nussinow blogs at TheVeggieQueen.com and is the author of *Vegan Under Pressure*.

Tofu Ramen Bowls

Slurping a steaming bowl of noodles in a garlicky, gingery stock is sublimely satisfying on a cold winter night. This Japanese favourite is so easy to make, serve it any night of the week.

PREP TIME	FUNCTION	CLOSED POT TIME	TOTAL TIME	RELEASE
30 minutes	Pressure/Manual (High)	40 minutes	1 hour 10 minutes + 4 hours marinate	Natural

SERVES: 2

- 6 tablespoons mirin
- 6 tablespoons low-salt soy sauce
- 2 tablespoons rice vinegar
- 1 tablespoon toasted sesame oil
- 2 teaspoons Asian chilli sauce, such as sriracha
- 3 tablespoons minced fresh ginger
- 2 tablespoons minced garlic
- 1 225-g block extra-firm tofu
- 950 ml vegetable stock
- 1 tablespoon minced garlic
- 3 tablespoons red miso

GARNISHES

Shredded cabbage

Hard-cooked eggs

Chopped spring onions

Thinly sliced daikon radish

Peeled and thinly sliced cucumber

- 1 300-g packet ready-to-eat Asian ramen noodles

PREP

In a medium bowl combine mirin, 3 tablespoons of the soy sauce, the rice vinegar, sesame oil, chilli sauce, 1 tablespoon of the ginger root and 1 tablespoon of the garlic. Mix well. Add the tofu, turning to cover with marinade. Cover bowl with cling film; let tofu marinate at room temperature for 4 to 6 hours. Remove tofu from marinade and transfer to a cutting board. Cut tofu into ½×2.5-cm rectangles. Cover and set aside.

Combine stock, remaining soy sauce, ginger root and garlic. Secure the lid on the pot. Close the pressure-release valve.

COOK

Select **MANUAL** and cook at high pressure for 5 minutes. When cooking is complete, use a natural release to depressurise.

SERVE

Whisk miso into the hot stock, stirring until it melts.

Ladle stock into large bowls. Garnish ramen bowls as desired with cabbage, halved hard-cooked eggs, spring onions, daikon radish, cucumber, noodles and tofu.

Creamy Split Pea & Bacon Soup

Simple and satisfying, this old-fashioned, creamy green soup is good – and good for you.

PREP TIME	FUNCTION	CLOSED POT TIME	TOTAL TIME	RELEASE
20 minutes	Sauté (Normal); Pressure/Manual (High)	50 minutes	1 hour 10 minutes	Natural

SERVES: 4 to 6

- 5 slices bacon or 100 g pancetta, chopped
- 1 medium onion, diced
- 1 celery stalk, diced
- 1 carrot, large diced
- 400 g dried green split peas, rinsed
- 1.5 litres water
- 1 bay leaf
- 1 teaspoon sea salt

PREP

Select **SAUTÉ** on the Instant Pot® and adjust to **NORMAL**. Add the bacon to the pot. When the fat begins to render and bacon begins to fry in the fat, stir until crispy. Using a slotted spoon, remove the bacon to a kitchen paper-lined plate, leaving any remaining fat in the pot; set aside.

Add the onion, celery and carrot to the pot. Sauté in the bacon fat until the onions have softened for about 5 minutes, scraping up any browned bits that have formed on the bottom of the inner pot. Press **CANCEL**.

Add split peas, the water, bay leaf and salt; stir to combine. Secure the lid on the pot. Close the pressure-release valve.

COOK

Select **MANUAL** and cook at high pressure for 5 minutes. When cooking is complete, use a natural release to depressurise.

SERVE

Remove and discard the bay leaf. Stir half of the bacon into the soup. Serve the soup topped with remaining bacon bits.

Laura Pazzaglia blogs at HipPressureCooking.com.

Chipotle Corn & Sweet Potato Chilli

The balance of sweetness from the corn and sweet potato and the smoky, spicy flavour of chipotle gives this vegetarian chilli great appeal.

PREP TIME	FUNCTION	CLOSED POT TIME	TOTAL TIME	RELEASE
35 minutes	Sauté (Normal); Pressure/Manual (High)	1 hour 20 minutes	1 hour 55 minutes	Natural

SERVES: 6 to 8

- 2 tablespoons olive oil
- 1 onion, chopped
- 1 red pepper, chopped
- 1 green pepper, chopped
- 1 jalapeño pepper, seeded (if desired) and finely chopped
- 4 cloves garlic, minced
- ½ teaspoon salt
- 75 g tomato paste
- 2 400-g pots vegetable or chicken stock
- 450 g diced sweet potatoes
- 125 g cooked black beans, pinto beans or kidney beans or two 425-g tins black beans, pinto beans or kidney beans, drained and rinsed
- 1 400-g tin diced tomatoes
- 175 g frozen corn
- 1 chipotle chilli from a jar, minced
- 2 tablespoons chilli powder
- 1½ teaspoons ground cumin
- 1 teaspoon dried oregano

  Grated cheddar cheese, chopped spring onions and/or chopped fresh coriander

PREP
Select **SAUTÉ** on the Instant Pot® and add olive oil to pot. When oil is hot, add onion, sweet peppers, jalapeño and garlic. Season with salt. Cook and stir until softened for about 5 minutes. Add tomato paste. Cook and stir for 1 minute. Press **CANCEL**. Add the stock, sweet potatoes, beans, tomatoes, corn, chipotle pepper, chilli powder, cumin and oregano.

Secure the lid on the pot. Close the pressure-release valve.

COOK
Select **MANUAL** and cook on high pressure for 30 minutes. When cooking is complete, use a natural release to depressurise.

SERVE
Serve chilli with cheese, spring onions and/or coriander.

Creamy Tomato Soup with Lemon & Basil

Lemon and fresh basil give this favourite soup a completely new flavour dimension. Serve it with toasty grilled cheese (of course!) and a glass of wine.

PREP TIME	FUNCTION	CLOSED POT TIME	TOTAL TIME	RELEASE
25 minutes	Sauté (Normal); Pressure/Manual (High)	50 minutes	1 hour 15 minutes	Natural

SERVES: 4 to 6

- 60 g butter
- 2 large leeks or 4 small leeks, halved lengthwise, rinsed and sliced (white and light green parts only)
- 2 cloves garlic, minced
- 1 175-g tin tomato paste
- 950 ml chicken stock
- 1 800-g tin whole tomatoes, undrained and cut up
- 1 tablespoon honey or sugar
- 240 ml double cream
- 20 g chopped fresh basil
- 2 tablespoons lemon juice
- 1 teaspoon lemon zest

PREP

Select **SAUTÉ** on the Instant Pot® and adjust to **NORMAL**. Add butter to pot. When the butter is melted, add the leeks. Cook, stirring occasionally, until leeks are softened for about 3 minutes. Stir in garlic. Cook for 2 minutes more. Stir in the tomato paste. Cook and stir for 1 minute. Press **CANCEL**. Stir in the chicken stock, tomatoes and honey. Secure the lid on the pot. Close the pressure-release valve.

COOK

Select **MANUAL** and cook at high pressure for 5 minutes. When cooking is complete, use a natural release to depressurise.

SERVE

Use an immersion blender to blend soup until smooth (or blend in a blender). Stir in cream, basil, lemon juice and lemon zest.

Smoky Butternut Bisque

Choose any non-dairy milk you like to add creaminess to this vegan soup. Almond, soy, coconut and cashew are all good choices.

PREP TIME	FUNCTION	CLOSED POT TIME	TOTAL TIME	RELEASE
10 minutes	Sauté (Normal); Pressure/Manual (High)	20 minutes	30 minutes	Quick

SERVES: 4

- 300 g chopped onions
- 900 g butternut squash, peeled, halved and seeds removed, cut into chunks
- 6 cloves garlic
- 2 pears, stems removed, halved and cored
- 1 tablespoon smoked paprika
- 1½ teaspoons salt-free seasoning
- ⅛ teaspoon chipotle powder
- 240 ml plain unsweetened non-dairy milk

PREP

Select **SAUTÉ** on the Instant Pot® and adjust to **NORMAL**. When hot, add the onions to the pot. Sauté the onions until browned, adding water if necessary. Add the squash, garlic, pears, paprika, seasoning and chipotle powder. Press **CANCEL**. Secure the lid on the pot. Close the pressure-release valve.

COOK

Select **MANUAL** and cook at high pressure for 6 minutes. When cooking is complete, use a quick release to depressurise.

SERVE

Add the milk and puree soup in a blender or in the pot using an immersion blender.

Chef AJ blogs at EatUnprocessed.com.

Curried Cauliflower Soup

Mild-mannered cauliflower takes beautifully to the intensity of the Thai red curry that flavours this soup. A tablespoon of honey tempers the heat just a bit.

PREP TIME	FUNCTION	CLOSED POT TIME	TOTAL TIME	RELEASE
25 minutes	Sauté (Normal); Pressure/Manual (High)	45 minutes	1 hour 10 minutes	Natural

SERVES: 6

- 2 tablespoons vegetable oil
- 1 medium onion, chopped
- 2 cloves garlic, minced
- 1 tablespoon minced fresh ginger
- 1 teaspoon ground cumin
- ½ teaspoon ground turmeric
- 2 tablespoons red curry paste
- 1 teaspoon finely grated lemon zest
- 1 large head cauliflower, broken into small florets
- 480 ml vegetable stock or chicken stock
- 360 ml chilled coconut milk at room temperature
- 1 tablespoon honey
- ½ teaspoon salt
- ¼ teaspoon black pepper
- 25 g chopped coriander

PREP

Select **SAUTÉ** on the Instant Pot® and adjust to **NORMAL**. Add oil to pot. When hot, add the onion. Cook and stir for 3 minutes or until tender. Stir in garlic and ginger. Cook and stir for 1 minute more. Add cumin, turmeric, curry paste and lemon zest. Cook and stir for 30 seconds. Press **CANCEL**. Add cauliflower florets and stock. Secure the lid on the pot. Close the pressure-release valve.

COOK

Select **MANUAL** and cook at high pressure for 5 minutes. When cooking is complete, use a natural release to depressurise.

SERVE

While cauliflower cooks, in a small bowl combine coconut milk, honey, salt and pepper. Blend thoroughly. Set aside.

In a food processor or blender puree cauliflower-stock mixture, in batches (or use an immersion blender in the pot). Transfer pureed mixture to a bowl and keep warm. Whisk in coconut milk mixture.

Ladle hot soup into warmed bowls. Sprinkle each serving with coriander.

Corn Chowder

The consummate soup of summer, this is best made when sweetcorn is in season – but if you're craving it in the dead of winter, it's very tasty made with frozen corn as well.

PREP TIME	FUNCTION	CLOSED POT TIME	TOTAL TIME	RELEASE
40 minutes	Sauté (Normal); Soup/Stock	1 hour	1 hour 40 minutes	Natural

SERVES: 6

4	slices bacon, chopped
140	g chopped onion
85	g chopped red sweet pepper
25	g chopped celery
2	cloves garlic, minced
1	teaspoon salt
¼	teaspoon black pepper
450	g Yukon gold potatoes, peeled and diced
950	ml chicken stock
525	g fresh corn kernels or frozen corn, thawed
240	ml double cream
1	teaspoon chopped fresh thyme

PREP

Select **SAUTÉ** on the Instant Pot® and adjust to **NORMAL**. Add bacon to pot. Cook bacon until crisp; remove with a slotted spoon to a kitchen paper-lined plate; set aside. Add onion, pepper, celery, garlic, salt and black pepper to bacon drippings in pot. Cook for 3 to 5 minutes until vegetables are softened, stirring frequently. Press **CANCEL**.

Add potatoes and chicken stock. Secure the lid on the pot. Close the pressure-release valve.

COOK

Select **SOUP/STOCK**. When cooking is complete, use a natural release to depressurise. Press **CANCEL**.

Select **SAUTÉ** and adjust to **NORMAL**. Bring soup to a simmer; add corn and cook for 3 to 5 minutes until tender. Press **CANCEL**.

SERVE

Stir in cream and thyme. Season to taste with salt and black pepper. Serve topped with bacon.

Carrot-Ginger Soup

This light and refreshing soup can be served warm or cold. It's lovely in both autumn and spring – when gardens and farmers markets are bursting with the sweet orange roots.

PREP TIME	FUNCTION		CLOSED POT TIME	TOTAL TIME	RELEASE
30 minutes	Soup/Stock		50 minutes	1 hour 20 minutes	Natural

SERVES: 6

- 710 ml chicken stock or vegetable stock
- 1 large onion, peeled and cut into 8 wedges
- 3 cloves garlic, peeled and smashed
- 2 tablespoons finely grated fresh ginger
- 450 g fresh carrots, peeled and cut into thirds
- 1 large golden potato, peeled and quartered
- 240 ml chilled coconut milk
- 3 tablespoons freshly squeezed lime juice
- 2 teaspoons finely grated lime zest
- Plain yogurt (optional)
- Snipped fresh chives (optional)

PREP
Combine stock, onion, garlic, ginger, carrots and potato in Instant Pot®.

Secure the lid on the pot. Close the pressure-release valve.

COOK
Select **SOUP/STOCK** and adjust cook time to 8 minutes. When cooking is complete, use a natural release to depressurise.

SERVE
Use an immersion blender to blend soup until smooth. (If using a blender or food processor, return all soup to pot.) Stir in coconut milk, lime juice and lime zest. Serve immediately garnished, if desired, with a dollop of yogurt and chives.

French Onion Soup

The key to perfect onion soup is allowing the natural sugars in the onions to infuse the beef stock with sweetness. The Instant Pot® does that in a fraction of the time of the traditional cooking method for this French favourite.

PREP TIME	FUNCTION	CLOSED POT TIME	TOTAL TIME	RELEASE
25 minutes	Sauté (Normal); Soup/Stock	50 minutes	1 hour 15 minutes + 5 minutes bake	Quick

SERVES: 4 to 6

CHEESE CROUTONS

950 ml 4-cm bread cubes (cut from Italian country loaf)

1 tablespoon olive oil

½ teaspoon garlic powder

55 g grated Gruyère cheese

25 g grated Parmesan cheese

SOUP

2 tablespoons olive oil

900 g sweet onions, sliced 0.5-cm thick

1 teaspoon salt

180 ml cream sherry

1..5 litres reduced-salt beef stock

3 sprigs fresh thyme

1 bay leaf

Salt and black pepper

PREP

For the croutons, preheat oven to 190°C/375°F. Place bread cubes in a large mixing bowl; drizzle with olive oil and toss to evenly distribute. Place on a foil-lined baking sheet that has been sprayed with non-stick cooking spray. Sprinkle with garlic powder. Set aside.

For the soup, select **SAUTÉ** on the Instant Pot® and adjust to **NORMAL**. Add 2 tablespoons olive oil to the pot. When hot, add onions and salt. Sauté for 3 minutes, stirring frequently. Add sherry and cook for an additional 4 minutes. Press **CANCEL**. Add beef stock, thyme and bay leaf. Secure the lid on the pot. Close the pressure-release valve.

COOK

Select **SOUP/STOCK**. When cooking is complete, use a quick release to depressurise.

SERVE

Combine both types of cheese and sprinkle over bread cubes. Bake for 5 to 7 minutes until cheese is melted and bubbly. Season soup with salt and pepper to taste. Divide soup among bowls. Top with warm cheese croutons.

Potato-Leek Soup

Velvety and delicately flavoured, this creamy soup makes a lovely first course for a nice dinner party – or a yummy lunch accompanied by a roast beef sandwich.

PREP TIME	FUNCTION	CLOSED POT TIME	TOTAL TIME	RELEASE
20 minutes	Sauté (Normal/Less); Soup/Stock	1 hour 5 minutes	1 hour 25 minutes + 5 minutes	Natural

SERVES: 6

- 2 tablespoons butter
- 2 large leeks, halved lengthwise, rinsed and thinly sliced (white and light green parts only)
- 1 teaspoon salt
- ¼ teaspoon black pepper
- 45 g russet potatoes, peeled and diced
- 950 ml chicken stock
- 240 ml double cream
- 2 tablespoons chopped fresh chives

PREP

Select **SAUTÉ** on the Instant Pot® and adjust to **NORMAL**. Melt butter in pot; add leeks, salt and pepper to pot. Cook for about 5 minutes or until leeks are softened, stirring frequently. Press **CANCEL**. Add potatoes and chicken stock. Secure the lid on the pot. Close the pressure-release valve.

COOK

Select **SOUP/STOCK**. When cooking is complete, use a natural release to depressurise. Press **CANCEL**.

SERVE

Blend soup in pot with an immersion blender or blend in a blender in small batches until smooth; return to pot. Stir in cream.

Select **SAUTÉ** and adjust to **LESS**. Bring soup just to a simmer (do not boil) for about 5 minutes. Stir in chives and season to taste with additional salt and pepper. Press **CANCEL**.

Simple Seafood Bouillabaisse

The ingredients list may look a little daunting, but the recipe is structured in such a way that you're prepping ingredients while the pot is cooking, making this elegant French stew infinitely doable.

PREP TIME	FUNCTION	CLOSED POT TIME	TOTAL TIME	RELEASE
10 minutes	Pressure/Manual (High); Sauté (Normal)	30 minutes	40 minutes	Quick

SERVES: 6

- 1 **medium fresh or frozen lobster tail (225 g to 300 g)**
- 350 **g fresh or frozen jumbo prawns**
- 350 **g fresh or frozen skinless halibut or sea bass, cut 2 cm to 4 cm thick**
- 1 **medium fennel bulb**
- 1 **medium red pepper, coarsely chopped**
- 1 **medium red onion, chopped**
- 1 **400-g tin diced tomatoes**
- 3 **cloves garlic, halved**
- 3 **wide, long strips orange zest (orange-colour outer part of the peel only)**
- 710 **ml seafood stock**
- 225 **g fresh mussels (see Tip, page 137)**
- 120 **ml dry white wine**
- ½ **teaspoon dried saffron threads, crushed**
- ¼ **teaspoon chilli flakes**
- 1½ **teaspoons chopped fresh flat-leaf parsley**
- 2 **tablespoons chopped fresh chives**
- **Lemon wedges**

PREP

Thaw lobster, prawns and halibut if frozen. Set aside. Trim tops off fennel bulb; reserve the tops for garnish if desired. Trim a thin slice off the bottom of the bulb; cut bulb in half. Cut out the core and discard. Chop the bulb; add to the Instant Pot®. Add pepper, onion, undrained tomatoes, garlic and orange zest. Rinse lobster tail with cold water; place lobster tail on top vegetables in the pot. Pour 240ml of the seafood stock over everything in pot.

COOK

Secure the lid on the pot. Close the pressure-release valve. Select **MANUAL** and cook at high pressure for 3 minutes. Once cooking is complete, use a quick release to depressurise. Transfer lobster tail to a cutting board. Transfer vegetables and cooking juices from the pot to a blender or food processor. If necessary, allow mixture to cool for about 10 minutes.* Cover and blend or process vegetable mixture until smooth. Set aside.

While lobster is cooking, clean mussels (see Tip, page 137). Peel and devein prawns. Rinse prawns and halibut with cold water; pat dry with kitchen paper. Cut halibut into 4-cm cubes. Add mussels, prawns and halibut to the pot. Pour remaining 470 ml seafood stock over everything. Secure the lid on the pot. Close the pressure-release valve. Select **MANUAL** and cook at high pressure for 2 minutes. Once cooking is complete, use a quick release to depressurise. Press **CANCEL**.

Using kitchen scissors, cut the lobster tail down the centre, along the soft side of the shell. Open the shell and remove the lobster meat. Chop lobster meat.

Add pureed vegetable mixture, lobster, wine, saffron and chilli flakes to the seafood mixture in the pot. Select **SAUTÉ** and adjust to **NORMAL**. Cook for 1 to 2 minutes or until heated through, stirring gently. Press **CANCEL**.

SERVE

Ladle into shallow bowls. If desired, snip some of the feathery tops of the reserved fennel. Sprinkle over each serving; sprinkle parsley and chives over each serving. Serve with lemon wedges.

***TIP:** Some blenders do not require liquid to be cool before blending. Check your blender manufacturer directions.

Desserts

Zinfandel-Poached Pears with Cinnamon Whipped Cream

This is an ideal dessert for entertaining because it has to be made far ahead of serving time. The overnight soak in the spiced wine syrup allows the flavour to deeply penetrate the pears.

PREP TIME	FUNCTION	CLOSED POT TIME	TOTAL TIME	RELEASE
15 minutes	Sauté (Normal); Pressure/Manual (High)	15 minutes	30 minutes + overnight chill	Quick

SERVES: 4

- 1 750-ml bottle medium-quality Zinfandel wine
- 100 g sugar
- Juice from 1 large navel orange (about 80 ml)
- 1 strip orange zest, about 5 cm wide by 8 cm long
- 1 cinnamon stick
- 3 whole cloves
- 3 whole allspice berries
- 4 firm, ripe pears

CINNAMON WHIPPED CREAM

- 300 ml whipping cream
- 50 g sugar
- ½ teaspoon ground cinnamon

PREP

Combine wine, sugar, orange juice, orange zest, cinnamon stick, cloves and berries in the Instant Pot®. Select **SAUTÉ** and adjust to **NORMAL**. Allow wine mixture to come to boiling, stirring to dissolve sugar.

While wine mixture cooks, peel pears, taking care that fruit is smooth and retains its shape. Do not remove stems. Cut a 1-cm slice from the bottom of each pear to make it stand upright. When sugar has dissolved, press **CANCEL**. Gently turn pears in wine mixture to coat, then arrange upright in mixture. Secure the lid on the pot. Close the pressure-release valve.

COOK

Select **MANUAL** and cook at high pressure for 5 minutes. When cooking is complete, use a quick release to depressurise. Press **CANCEL**. Open lid; carefully remove the pears to a bowl. Pour wine mixture over the pears. Cover and transfer to fridge. Let wine-immersed pears chill for at least 12 hours, turning pears in mixture a few times during chilling time.

Using a slotted spoon, gently remove pears from wine mixture and transfer them to serving plates.

Transfer wine mixture to pot, select **SAUTÉ** And adjust to **NORMAL**. Cook and stir wine syrup over medium heat for 12 to 15 minutes or until mixture is syrupy. Press **CANCEL**.

SERVE

While syrup is simmering, prepare Cinnamon Whipped Cream: In the chilled bowl of an electric mixer beat cream on high speed until soft peaks form. With mixer running, slowly sprinkle cream with sugar and cinnamon. Continue beating until stiff peaks form.

Spoon syrup over pears. Serve generous dollops of Cinnamon Whipped Cream alongside poached pears.

Raspberry-Vanilla Bean Rice Pudding

It's slightly more time-consuming to split and scrape the vanilla bean than to simply measure out vanilla extract, but the more intense flavour is worth a little bit of fuss – and you get the beautiful speckles from the vanilla bean seeds in the pudding.

PREP TIME	FUNCTION	CLOSED POT TIME	TOTAL TIME	RELEASE
10 minutes	Sauté (Normal); Porridge	45 minutes	55 minutes	Natural

SERVES: 6

240 ml water

480 ml milk

50 g sugar

3 tablespoons seedless raspberry jam

225 g Arborio rice or other desired white rice

1 cinnamon stick

1 vanilla bean, halved lengthwise, or 1 teaspoon vanilla extract

250 g fresh raspberries

120 ml double cream

PREP
Select **SAUTÉ** on the Instant Pot® and adjust to **NORMAL**. Add the water, milk, sugar and jam to the pot. Cook and stir until sugar and jam dissolve. Press **CANCEL**. Stir in the rice and cinnamon stick. Split the vanilla bean with the tip of a small sharp knife and scrape the seeds into the pot. Add the bean to the pot. Secure the lid on the pot. Close the pressure-release valve.

COOK
Select **PORRIDGE**. When cooking is complete, use a natural release to depressurise.

SERVE
Remove and discard vanilla bean and cinnamon stick. Stir in fresh raspberries and cream.

Chocolate-Cherry Croissant Bread Pudding

Chocolate and cherries complement each other very well. Although dried tart cherries are more common, look for dried sweet cherries to make this decadent bread pudding. They are often available in bulk at health-food stores, in supermarkets or online.

PREP TIME	FUNCTION	CLOSED POT TIME	TOTAL TIME	RELEASE
15 minutes	Manual/Pressure (High)	35 minutes	1 hour 10 minutes + 20 minutes cool	Natural

SERVES: 6

- 480 ml water
- 1 tablespoon butter, softened
- 2 eggs, beaten
- 100 g sugar
- 480 ml single cream
- 1 teaspoon vanilla extract
- 250 g 2.5-cm day-old croissant pieces
- 40 g dried sweet cherries
- 60 g chopped bittersweet chocolate

PREP

Place trivet in the Instant Pot®. Add the water to the pot. Butter a 1.5-litre soufflé dish or casserole that fits in pot.

Whisk together eggs, sugar, cream and vanilla in a medium bowl. Add croissant pieces and cherries; let stand for 10 minutes. Stir in chocolate and transfer mixture to prepared dish. Cover dish with foil and place on trivet. Secure the lid on the pot. Close the pressure-release valve.

COOK

Select **MANUAL** and cook at high pressure 15 minutes. When cooking is complete, use a natural release to depressurise.

SERVE

Carefully remove dish from pot. Remove foil and let cool for 20 minutes before serving.

Chamomile-Cherry-Poached Peaches

The window for making this dessert is fleeting–peach season doesn't last more than a couple of months in late summer and early autumn, so seize the opportunity while you can. The chamomile infuses the wine syrup with a subtle floral flavour.

PREP TIME	FUNCTION	CLOSED POT TIME	TOTAL TIME	RELEASE
5 minutes	Sauté (Normal); Pressure/Manual (High)	10 minutes	50 minutes + 6 hours chill	Quick

SERVES: 4

- 980 ml pink Moscato wine
- 100 g sugar
- 120 g dried tart cherries, chopped
- 2 100%-chamomile tea bags, tags removed
- 2 tablespoons freshly squeezed lemon juice
- 4 small firm, ripe peaches, washed, halved and pitted
- 110 g plain Greek yogurt
- 110 g shelled, salted pistachio nuts, coarsely chopped

PREP

Combine wine, sugar, cherries, tea bags and lemon juice in the Instant Pot®. Select **SAUTÉ** and adjust to **NORMAL**. Bring mixture to boiling. Press **CANCEL**. Add peach halves, skin sides up, to the pot.

Secure the lid on the pot. Close the pressure-release valve.

COOK

Select **MANUAL** and cook at high pressure for 2 minutes. When cooking is complete, use a quick release to depressurise. Press **CANCEL**.

Using a slotted spoon, gently transfer peaches to a shallow dish and let cool. When cool, cover lightly and chill for at least 6 hours. (Remove skin from peaches before chilling if desired.)

While peaches are cooling, select **SAUTÉ** and adjust to **NORMAL**. Bring liquid in pot to boiling and let mixture simmer, stirring often, for about 12 to 15 minutes or until liquid has a syrupy consistency. Remove and discard tea bags. Press **CANCEL**.

Transfer inner pot to a cooling rack and let syrup cool for 15 minutes. Transfer to a covered container and chill in the fridge alongside peaches.

SERVE

To serve, place two peach halves on each plate. Drizzle syrup over peaches. Garnish each peach half with a small dollop of Greek yogurt; sprinkle with pistachios.

Chocolate, Orange & Olive Oil Mini Lava Cake

This warm chocolate dessert is made almost entirely with ingredients you have in your cupboards, so it's perfect for satisfying those spur-of-the-moment chocolate cravings. If you don't have an orange, substitute ¼ teaspoon vanilla extract for the ½ teaspoon zest.

PREP TIME	FUNCTION	CLOSED POT TIME	TOTAL TIME	RELEASE
10 minutes	Pressure/Manual (High)	20 minutes	30 minutes + 5 minutes stand	Quick

SERVES: 2 (1 mug)

- 240 ml water
- 90 g flour
- ½ teaspoon orange zest
- 50 g sugar
- Pinch of salt
- 1 tablespoon unsweetened cocoa powder
- ½ teaspoon baking powder
- 1 egg
- 60 ml milk
- 2 tablespoons extra virgin olive oil, plus additional for greasing mug

PREP

Place the trivet in the Instant Pot®. Add the water to the Instant Pot. Coat a 350-g coffee mug, tea cup or ramekin with olive oil.

Combine flour, orange zest, sugar, salt, cocoa and baking powder in a 475-ml measuring cup. Mix with a fork. Add the egg, milk and the 2 tablespoons olive oil. Mix until a batter forms. Pour the batter into the prepared cup. Place the cup in the pot. If you are making more than one cup, arrange them so they are straight and not touching the inside of the pot. Secure the lid on the pot. Close the pressure-release valve.

COOK

Select **MANUAL** and cook at high pressure for 15 minutes. When cooking is complete, use a quick release to depressurise.

SERVE

Let stand for 5 minutes before serving. (Or, for a gooey centre, serve immediately. The cake will continue cooking as you let it rest, so the interior will solidify.)

Laura Pazzaglia blogs at HipPressureCooking.com.

Vegan Pear & Cranberry Cake

Rustic and not overly sweet, this wholegrain autumn fruit cake is actually good for you! Not a bad deal for dessert.

PREP TIME	FUNCTION	CLOSED POT TIME	TOTAL TIME	RELEASE
20 minutes	Pressure/Manual (High)	1 hour 15 minutes	1 hour 35 minutes	Natural

SERVES: 6 to 8

Vegetable oil

175 g whole wheat pastry flour (or use gluten-free baking mix)

½ teaspoon ground cardamom

½ teaspoon bicarbonate of soda

½ teaspoon baking powder

2 tablespoons ground flaxseeds

⅛ teaspoon salt

120 ml plain unsweetened non-dairy milk

2 tablespoons agave nectar

½ teaspoon liquid stevia

2 tablespoons vegetable oil (or apple sauce to make oil-free)

225 g chopped pear

50 g chopped fresh cranberries

360 ml water

PREP

Oil a 15-cm to 18-cm bundt tin and set aside. Stir together the flour, cardamom, bicarbonate of soda, baking powder, flax and salt in a bowl. In a large measuring cup mix together the milk, sweetener and oil. Add the wet ingredients to the dry ingredients and mix well. Fold in the pear and cranberries.

Spread the batter into the prepared tin and cover with foil. Place the trivet in the pot. Pour the water into the Instant Pot®. Place the tin on the trivet. Secure the lid on the pot. Close the pressure-release valve.

COOK

Select **MANUAL** and cook at high pressure for 35 minutes. When cooking is complete, use a natural release to depressurise.

SERVE

Carefully lift the tin out of the pot and remove the foil. Let cool on a cake rack completely before removing the cake from the tin and/or cutting.

*TIP: If you can't find this product, substitute 2 tablespoons agave nectar and ½ teaspoon liquid stevia.

Kathy Hester is the creator of HealthySlowCooking.com and author of *The Ultimate Vegan Cookbook for Your Instant Pot®.*

Peanut Butter-Chocolate Bundt Cake

A much-loved flavour combination shines in this super-moist and rich cake. Choose your glaze – either chocolate or peanut butter – or, if you can't decide, make both.

PREP TIME	FUNCTION	CLOSED POT TIME	TOTAL TIME	RELEASE
25 minutes	Manual/Pressure (High)	35 minutes	1 hour + 2 hours cool	Quick

SERVES: 8

Non-stick baking spray

50 **g bittersweet chocolate, chopped**

60 **g plain flour**

½ **teaspoon baking powder**

¼ **teaspoon salt**

110 **g butter, softened**

100 **g sugar**

2 **eggs**

1 **teaspoon vanilla extract**

40 **g creamy peanut butter**

240 **ml water**

Ganache or Peanut Butter Glaze

Chopped honey-roasted peanuts (optional)

GANACHE

60 **ml whipping cream**

75 **g milk, semisweet or plain chocolate, chopped**

PEANUT BUTTER GLAZE

25 **g icing sugar**

3 **tablespoons creamy peanut butter**

2 **tablespoons to 3 tablespoons milk**

PREP
Generously coat a 3-cup fluted Bundt pan (available online) with baking spray. In a small saucepan melt the chocolate over low heat. Set aside to cool.

In a small bowl stir together the flour, baking powder and salt; set aside. In a medium bowl beat the butter on medium speed for 30 seconds. Add the sugar and beat on medium for 1 to 2 minutes or until well combined. Add the eggs, one at a time, beating well after each addition. Beat in the vanilla. Add flour mixture and beat just until combined. Transfer half of the batter to a small bowl; stir in the melted chocolate. Stir peanut butter into the remaining batter.

Alternately drop spoonfuls of chocolate and peanut butter batters into the prepared pan. Using a table knife, gently cut through batters to swirl them together (do not overmix).

Place the trivet in the Instant Pot®. Add the water to pot. Place the cake tin on the trivet. Secure the lid on the pot. Close the pressure-release valve.

COOK
Select **MANUAL** and cook at high pressure for 25 minutes. When cooking is complete, use a quick release to depressurise.

SERVE
Carefully remove the cake from the pot. Let the cake cool on a wire rack for 10 minutes, then remove cake from tin and let cool completely on a wire rack. Drizzle with Ganache or Peanut Butter Glaze. If using Peanut Butter Glaze, sprinkle with peanuts if desired.

GANACHE: In a small saucepan bring whipping cream just to boiling over medium heat. Remove from heat and add the chocolate. Do not stir. Let stand for 5 minutes. Stir until smooth. Cool for 15 minutes before using.

PEANUT BUTTER GLAZE: In a small bowl stir together the icing sugar, peanut butter and enough milk to make a thick drizzling consistency.

Mocha Pots de Crème

Coffee and cocoa come together in this silky custard. Pronounced POH-duh-KREM (think fancy French dessert), it can be made in the morning and chilled all day before serving.

PREP TIME	FUNCTION	CLOSED POT	TOTAL TIME	RELEASE
15 minutes	Sauté (Normal); Pressure/Manual (High)	15 minutes	30 minutes + 20 minutes cool + 3 hours chill	Quick

SERVES: 4

- ½ teaspoon espresso powder
- ½ teaspoon vanilla extract
- 285 ml single cream
- 75 g bittersweet chocolate, grated
- 50 g sugar
- 3 egg yolks
- 360 ml water
- Whipped cream (optional)
- Cinnamon (optional)

PREP

Combine espresso powder, vanilla and cream in the Instant Pot®. Whisk to dissolve espresso powder. Select **SAUTÉ** and adjust to **NORMAL**. Bring cream mixture just to boiling. Press **CANCEL** and stir in chocolate.

In a medium bowl combine sugar and egg yolks. Whisk until thick and well combined.

Ladle approximately 80 ml hot chocolate mixture into the egg mixture. Whisk well. Pour all of egg mixture into the chocolate mixture; mix until smooth.

Ladle custard into four 175-g ramekins; set aside. Remove inner pot and wash. Carefully cover pots de crème with foil.

Return clean inner pot to the cooker. Place trivet in the pot, tucking handles underneath. Add water to pot. Arrange three of the ramekins evenly on the trivet. Set remaining ramekin on top of the other three. Secure the lid on the pot. Close the pressure-release valve.

COOK

Select **MANUAL** and cook at high pressure for 6 minutes. When cooking is complete, use a quick release to depressurise.

SERVE

Carefully remove pots de crème from pot. Transfer to a wire rack. Cool for 20 minutes, then transfer to the fridge. Let chill for at least 3 hours.

To serve, remove foil from ramekins. If desired, top each dessert with a dollop of whipped cream and a sprinkle of cinnamon. Serve cold.

Crème Brûlée

If you have a kitchen torch, caramelise the sugar on top of the custards. If not, it can be done in a pan on the hob.

PREP TIME	FUNCTION	CLOSED POT TIME	TOTAL TIME	RELEASE
15 minutes	Pressure/Manual (High)	25 minutes	40 minutes + 30 minutes cool + 2 hours chill	Natural

SERVES: 3

320 ml whipping cream

3 tablespoons sugar

4 egg yolks

1 teaspoon pure vanilla extract

Dash salt

240 ml water

2 tablespoons sugar

PREP
In a medium bowl combine 80 ml of the whipping cream, the sugar, egg yolks, vanilla and salt. Whisk until well combined. Slowly whisk in the remaining 240 ml whipping cream until smooth. Evenly pour cream mixture into three 175 g custard cups or ramekins. Cover cups or ramekins with foil.

Place trivet in the bottom of the Instant Pot®; add the water to the pot. Arrange filled custard cups on the trivet. Secure the lid on the pot. Close the pressure-release valve.

COOK
Select **MANUAL** and cook at high pressure for 10 minutes. When cooking is complete, use a natural release to depressurise.

SERVE
Use pot holders to transfer custard cups to a wire rack; uncover cups. Let stand for 30 to 60 minutes or until completely cool. Cover; chill for at least 2 hours or for up to 3 days.

To serve, sprinkle 2 tablespoons sugar evenly over surface of the custards (use about 2 teaspoons sugar per custard). Using a small hand-held blow torch,* slowly and evenly melt the sugar, allowing it to turn a deep golden brown.

*TIP: If you don't have a blow torch, pour 2 tablespoons sugar into a heavy small frying pan. Heat sugar over medium-high heat until sugar begins to melt, shaking the pan occasionally for even melting. Do not stir. When sugar starts to melt, reduce heat to low; continue to cook until all sugar is melted and golden brown, stirring with a wooden spoon so all sugar melts evenly. Immediately pour the melted sugar over custards. If the sugar starts to harden in the pan, return to heat and stir until melted.

MAPLE-GINGER CRÈME BRÛLÉE: Prepare as directed except substitute 3 tablespoons pure maple syrup for the 3 tablespoons sugar and add ¼ teaspoon ground ginger with the salt. If desired, sprinkle tops of custards with 2 teaspoons finely chopped crystallised ginger just before serving.

Raspberry Cheesecake

Just a little bit of raspberry extract boosts the flavour of the filling of this cheesecake, but it's not crucial.

PREP TIME	FUNCTION	CLOSED POT TIME	TOTAL TIME	RELEASE
30 minutes	Pressure/Manual (High)	1 hour	1 hour 30 minutes + 1 hour cool + 4 hours chill	Natural

SERVES: 8

Non-stick cooking spray

100 g Oreo cookie crumbs (about 12 Oreos, filling removed)

2 tablespoons butter, melted

450 g cream cheese, softened

50 g sugar

1 tablespoon plain flour

¼ teaspoon raspberry extract (optional)

150 g seedless raspberry jam

60 ml soured cream

2 eggs, room temperature

Red food colouring (optional)

480 ml water

175 g milk chocolate, finely chopped

80 ml double cream

Fresh raspberries

PREP

Spray a 15-cm or 18-cm springform tin with non-stick spray. Cut a piece of baking parchment to fit the bottom of the tin. Place in tin and spray again; set aside. Combine cookie crumbs and butter in a bowl. Press into the bottom and 2.5 cm up the side of the pan. Place in the freezer for 10 minutes.

In a large bowl beat the cream cheese, sugar, flour and extract (if using) until smooth and creamy. Mix in the jam and soured cream. Add eggs, beating just until combined. Add a drop or two of red food colouring to tint to desired hue if desired. Stir gently until combined. Pour into prepared crust.

Pour the water into the Instant Pot®. Place the trivet in the bottom of the pot. Cut a piece of foil the same size as a piece of kitchen paper. Place the foil under the kitchen paper and place the tin on top of the kitchen paper. Wrap the bottom of the tin in the foil with the kitchen paper as a barrier.

Fold an 45-cm-long piece of foil into thirds lengthwise. Place under the pan and use the two sides as a sling to place cheesecake in the pot. Secure the lid on the pot. Close the pressure-release valve.

COOK

Select **MANUAL** and cook at high pressure for 35 minutes. When cooking is complete, use a natural pressure release to depressurise.

SERVE

Remove the cheesecake from the pot using the sling. Cool on a wire rack for 1 hour and then fridge for at least 4 hours. Carefully remove tin sides.

When cheesecake is chilled, prepare the topping: Place half the chocolate in a bowl. Heat cream in a small saucepan over medium-high heat until it comes to a boil. Remove from heat and immediately pour cream over chocolate, stirring until chocolate is completely melted. Add remaining chocolate and stir until completely melted. Cool until ganache is thickened but still thin enough to drip down the sides of the cheesecake.

Spoon ganache on top of cake, spreading to edges and letting it drip down sides. Decorate top of cake with raspberries. Chill until ready to serve.

Barbara Schieving is the creator of the blog PressureCookingToday.com.

Triple-Citrus Cheesecake

This is the lightest, fluffiest cheesecake you'll taste anywhere. The moist cooking environment in the Instant Pot® makes it super creamy and greatly reduces the chances it will crack or dry out. Be sure to beat the eggs just until combined to ensure the cake won't sink in the middle as it cools.

PREP TIME	FUNCTION	CLOSED POT TIME	TOTAL TIME	RELEASE
30 minutes	Manual/Pressure (High)	1 hour	1 hour 30 minutes + 1 hour cool + 4 hours chill	Natural

SERVES: 8

Non-stick cooking spray

255 g graham cracker or vanilla wafer crumbs

2 tablespoons sugar

4 tablespoons melted butter

450 g cream cheese, softened

100 g sugar

1 tablespoon flour

¼ teaspoon salt

2 teaspoons vanilla extract

2 tablespoons orange juice

2 eggs

½ teaspoon freshly grated orange zest

½ teaspoon freshly grated lemon zest

½ teaspoon freshly grated lime zest

480 ml water

Fresh orange segments (optional)

PREP

Lightly spray a 38-cm or 45-cm springform tin with cooking spray. Cut a piece of baking parchment to fit the bottom of the tin. Place in the tin and spray again; set aside.

Combine crackers, the 2 tablespoons sugar and butter in a bowl; mix well. Press into bottom and about 25 cm up the sides of the tin.

In a large bowl beat cream cheese, the 100 g sugar, flour, salt, vanilla and orange juice until smooth and creamy. Add eggs, beating just until combined. Stir in citrus zests. Pour into prepared crust.

Pour the water into the Instant Pot®. Place the trivet in the bottom of the pot. Cut a piece of foil the same size as a piece of kitchen paper. Place the foil under the kitchen paper and place the pan on top of the kitchen paper. Wrap the bottom of the tin in the foil, with the kitchen paper as a barrier.

Fold an 45-cm-long piece of foil into thirds lengthwise. Place under the tin and use the two sides as a sling to place cheesecake in the pot. Secure the lid on the pot. Close the pressure-release valve.

COOK

Select **MANUAL** and cook at high pressure for 35 minutes. When cooking is complete, use a natural pressure release to depressurise.

SERVE

Remove the cheesecake from the pot using the sling. Cool on a wire rack for 1 hour and then chill for at least 4 hours. Carefully remove tin sides. Top cheesecake with fresh orange segments if desired.

Sauces, Spreads & Jams

Quick & Easy Marinara Sauce

You can buy jarred sauce, but it doesn't taste as fresh as sauce you make yourself. By cooking it in the Instant Pot®, you not only you get rich flavour in the fraction of the time it takes to cook it on the hob, but there's no spattering, either!

PREP TIME	FUNCTION	CLOSED POT TIME	TOTAL TIME	RELEASE
20 minutes	Sauté (Normal); Pressure/Manual (High)	55 minutes	1 hour 15 minutes	Natural

MAKES: 2.25kg

- 3 tablespoons extra virgin olive oil
- 6 cloves garlic, minced
- 2 800-g tins whole tomatoes
- 2 425-g tins no-salt-added tomato sauce
- 60 ml water
- 2 teaspoons dried Italian mixed herbs
- ½ teaspoon salt
- ¼ teaspoon black pepper
- ⅛ teaspoon to ¼ teaspoon chilli flakes
- 10 g chopped fresh basil
- 1½ teaspoons chopped fresh flat-leaf parsley

PREP
Select **SAUTÉ** on the Instant Pot® and adjust to **NORMAL**. When hot, add 1 tablespoon of the oil and the garlic. Cook and stir for 10 to 20 seconds or until garlic is fragrant but not brown. Press **CANCEL**. Add undrained tomatoes, tomato sauce, the water, Italian dried herbs seasoning, salt, black pepper and chilli flakes to the pot. Secure the lid on the pot. Close the pressure-release valve.

COOK
Select **MANUAL** and cook at high pressure for 10 minutes. When cooking is complete, use a natural release to depressurise.

SERVE
Using a potato masher, mash sauce to desired consistency (or for a smooth sauce, use an immersion blender or regular blender to blend sauce until smooth). Stir in remaining olive oil, the basil and parsley. Serve as desired.

Chipotle Barbecue Sauce

If you don't want the touch of smoke and heat the chipotle brings to this sauce, simply leave it out.

PREP TIME	FUNCTION	CLOSED POT TIME	TOTAL TIME	RELEASE
20 minutes	Sauté (Normal); Pressure/Manual (High)	20 minutes	40 minutes + 5 minutes simmer	Quick

MAKES: 750g

1	tablespoon cooking oil
75	g finely chopped onion
2	cloves garlic, minced
335	g ketchup
240	ml water
70	g packed brown sugar
80	ml apple cider vinegar
2	tablespoons honey
1	chipotle chilli in adobo from a jar, finely chopped
2	teaspoons chilli powder
2	teaspoons Dijon mustard
¼	teaspoon black pepper

PREP

Select **SAUTÉ** on the Instant Pot® and adjust to **NORMAL**. Heat oil in pot; add onion and cook for 2 minutes or until softened, stirring frequently. Add garlic; cook and stir for 1 minute more. Press **CANCEL**.

Add ketchup, water, brown sugar, vinegar, honey, chipotle, chilli powder, mustard and black pepper; stir well. Secure the lid on the pot. Close the pressure-release valve.

COOK

Select **MANUAL** and cook at high pressure for 10 minutes. When cooking is complete, use a quick release to depressurise. Press **CANCEL**.

SERVE

For a thicker sauce, select **SAUTÉ** and adjust to **LESS**. Bring sauce to a simmer. Cook for 5 to 10 minutes or until mixture reaches desired consistency, stirring frequently. Press **CANCEL**.

Honey-Cinnamon Apple Sauce

This silky apple sauce is so delicious, you'll forget that it's actually good for you. Use a mix of apples for a more complex flavour.

PREP TIME	FUNCTION	CLOSED POT TIME	TOTAL TIME	RELEASE
10 minutes	Pressure/Manual (High)	45 minutes	55 minutes	Natural

MAKES: 1.35kg

1.8	kg apples, such as Golden Delicious, Pink Lady and/or Fuji
120	ml apple cider
120	ml water
60	ml honey
2	tablespoons lemon juice
3	cinnamon sticks
¼	teaspoon salt

PREP

Core, peel and chop the apples. Combine the apples, cider, the water, honey, lemon juice, cinnamon sticks and salt in the Instant Pot®. Secure the lid on the pot. Close the pressure-release valve.

COOK

Select **MANUAL** and cook at high pressure for 8 minutes. When cooking is complete, use a natural release to depressurise. Press **CANCEL**.

SERVE

Remove cinnamon sticks. Use a potato masher to mash the apple sauce or, working in batches, transfer to a food processor and process until smooth (or use an immersion blender in the pot).

If apple sauce is thin, select **SAUTÉ** and adjust to **LESS**. Cook and stir for 10 to 15 minutes or until desired consistency. Press **CANCEL**.

Bacon-Onion Jam

Sweet, smoky, salty and tangy, this mélange of caramelised onions and bacon is the perfect way to top a wheel of baked Brie or a burger. This recipe makes a fairly chunky jam. If you want it a little smoother, transfer the finished jam to a food processor and pulse a few times.

PREP TIME	FUNCTION	CLOSED POT TIME	TOTAL TIME
40 minutes	Sauté (Normal/Less); Slow Cook (Less)	6 hours	6 hours 40 minutes

MAKES: 1.2kg

450	g thick-cut bacon, diced into 1-cm pieces
3	large onions, halved and thinly sliced
3	garlic cloves, minced
110	g packed brown sugar
60	ml apple cider or apple juice
60	ml apple cider vinegar
1	teaspoon fresh thyme leaves
¼	teaspoon ground cinnamon
	Dash cayenne pepper

PREP

Add bacon to Instant Pot®. Select **SAUTÉ** and adjust to **NORMAL**. Cook and stir until bacon is cooked through but not crisp for about 8 minutes. Remove bacon to a kitchen paper-lined plate; chill. Remove all but 1 tablespoon of the bacon grease from the pot.

Add onions and garlic to drippings in the pot. Cook and stir for 5 minutes until just tender. Press **CANCEL**.

Add brown sugar, apple cider, vinegar, thyme, cinnamon and cayenne. Stir to combine. Secure the lid on the pot. Open the pressure-release valve.

COOK

Select **SLOW COOK** and adjust to **LESS**. Cook for 6 to 7 hours. Press **CANCEL**.

Add cooked bacon to pot. Select **SAUTÉ** and adjust to **LESS**. Cook jam until most of the liquid has been evaporated for 5 to 10 minutes. Press **CANCEL**.

STORE

Cool and chill for up to 1 week. (Jam can also be frozen.)

Orange Marmalade

Using a mandoline to slice the oranges will give you the thinnest, most even slices.

PREP TIME	FUNCTION	CLOSED POT TIME	TOTAL TIME	RELEASE
15 minutes	Pressure/Manual (High); Sauté (Normal)	40 minutes	55 minutes	Natural

MAKES: about 1.2kg

3 **medium oranges (about 675g)**

360 **ml water**

600 **g sugar**

PREP

Thinly slice the oranges, removing and discarding any seeds. Cut the orange slices into quarters. Add oranges and the water to the Instant Pot®. Secure the lid on the pot. Close the pressure-release valve.

COOK

Select **MANUAL** and cook at high pressure for 10 minutes. When cooking is complete, use a natural release to depressurise. Press **CANCEL**.

Remove the lid and stir in sugar. Select **SAUTÉ** and adjust to **NORMAL**. Bring mixture to a full boil. Boil for 5 to 10 minutes or until mixture reaches gel stage (110°C/220°F), stirring frequently. Press **CANCEL**.

STORE

Ladle into 300-ml glass jars. Seal jars. Store for up to 3 weeks in the fridge.

Apple Butter

Rich and fragrant with cinnamon and nutmeg, this old-school spread is delicious on a slice of warm buttered toast–especially if it's made with raisin-walnut bread.

PREP TIME	FUNCTION	CLOSED POT TIME	TOTAL TIME	RELEASE
25 minutes	Pressure/Manual (High); Sauté (Less)	45 minutes	1 hour 10 minutes + 10 minutes	Natural

MAKES: 6 or 7 300-ml jars

- 1.8 kg apples, such as Golden Delicious, Granny Smith, Gala and/or Braeburn, cored and chopped (peel on if desired)
- 60 ml apple cider
- 110 g packed brown sugar
- 100 g granulated sugar
- 2 teaspoons ground cinnamon
- ½ teaspoon ground nutmeg
- 1 teaspoon vanilla extract

PREP
Add apples, cider, brown sugar, granulated sugar, cinnamon and nutmeg to the Instant Pot®. Secure the lid on the pot. Close the pressure-release valve.

COOK
Select **MANUAL** and cook at high pressure for 8 minutes. When cooking is complete, use a natural release to depressurise. Press **CANCEL**.

Use a potato masher or immersion blender to blend the apples until fairly smooth. Select **SAUTÉ** and adjust to **LESS**. Simmer apple butter for 10 to 15 minutes or until thickened to desired consistency. Stir in the vanilla. Press **CANCEL**. Cool completely.

STORE
Transfer to 300-ml glass jars. Seal jars. Store for up to 3 weeks in the fridge or freeze for up to 3 months. (If frozen, it will have a thinner consistency upon thawing.)

Strawberry Jam

Fully ripe strawberries – sweet, juicy and red all of the way through – make the best jam. Visit a pick-your-own farm in late spring and early summer and give jam-making a whirl.

PREP TIME	FUNCTION	CLOSED POT TIME	TOTAL TIME	RELEASE
20 minutes	Sauté (Normal); Pressure/Manual (High)	40 minutes	1 hour	Natural

MAKES: about 900g

950 ml quartered fresh strawberries

500 g sugar

60 ml lemon juice

PREP
Combine strawberries, sugar and lemon juice in the Instant Pot®.

Select **SAUTÉ** and adjust to **NORMAL**. Bring mixture to a full boil for about 8 minutes, stirring frequently. Press **CANCEL**. Secure the lid on the pot. Close the pressure-release valve.

COOK
Select **MANUAL** and cook at high pressure for 8 minutes. When cooking is complete, use a natural release to depressurise. Press **CANCEL**.

Remove the lid. Mash berries with a potato masher. Select **SAUTÉ** and adjust to **NORMAL**. Bring mixture to a full boil. Boil for 5 minutes or until mixture reaches gel stage (110°C/220°F), stirring frequently. Press **CANCEL**.

STORE
Ladle into 300-ml glass jars. Seal jars. Store for up to 3 weeks in the fridge.

Strawberry-Rhubarb Sauce

Spoon this sweet-tart sauce over angel food cake, ice cream and waffles.

PREP TIME	FUNCTION	CLOSED POT TIME	TOTAL TIME
1 hour 10 minutes	Slow Cook (More)	1 hour 30 minutes	1 hour 40 minutes

MAKES: 675g

225 g 1-cm to 2-cm diced frozen or fresh rhubarb

450 g whole strawberries, stems removed, halved

50 g sugar

¼ teaspoon almond extract

1 teaspoon fresh lemon juice

PREP
Place rhubarb, strawberries and sugar in the Instant Pot®. Secure the lid on the pot. Open the pressure-release valve.

COOK
Select **SLOW COOK** and adjust to **MORE.** Cook for 1½ hours.

SERVE
When cooking is complete, mash berries and rhubarb with a fork or potato masher. Stir in almond extract and lemon juice; cool. Cover and chill before serving.

Cranberry Sauce with Apple Brandy

Don't settle for boring cranberry sauce. This version – spiced with orange, cardamom, cinnamon and maple syrup – is super simple to make and so much better than sauce from a jar.

PREP TIME	FUNCTION	CLOSED POT TIME	TOTAL TIME	RELEASE
20 minutes	Pressure/Manual (High); Sauté (Less)	30 minutes	50 minutes	Natural

MAKES: 750g

- 360 g fresh cranberries
- 250 g peeled, minced apple
- 60 ml orange juice (about 2 medium oranges)
- 1 tablespoon orange zest
- 10 cardamom pods
- 2 cinnamon sticks
- ¼ teaspoon salt
- 120 ml water
- 2 tablespoons apple brandy or spiced rum
- 2 to 4 tablespoons maple syrup or other sweetener
- ¼ teaspoon ground cardamom

PREP
Combine cranberries, apple, orange juice and zest, cardamom pods, cinnamon sticks, salt and the water in the Instant Pot®. Secure the lid on the pot. Close the pressure-release valve.

COOK
Select **MANUAL** and cook at high pressure for 6 minutes. When cooking is complete, use a natural release to depressurise. Press **CANCEL**.

Select **SAUTÉ** and adjust to **LESS**. Stir in the brandy, maple syrup and ground cardamom. Cook and mash the fruit pieces. Cook until sauce reaches desired consistency. Press **CANCEL**.

SERVE
Remove the cardamom pods and cinnamon sticks. Store in a tightly sealed container in the fridge for up to 1 week.

Kathy Hester is the creator of HealthySlowCooking.com and the author of *The Ultimate Vegan Cookbook for Your Instant Pot®*.

Mango-Ginger Chutney

The combination of heat and sweet is classic in mango chutney. How much heat it has is up to you–just vary the amount of chilli flakes according to your taste. To seed a mango, stand it on its end and slice down either side of the large seed, discarding the centre that contains the seed.

PREP TIME	FUNCTION		CLOSED POT TIME	TOTAL TIME	RELEASE
25 minutes	Pressure/High; Sauté (Less)		30 minutes	55 minutes	Natural

MAKES: 90 g

- 4 ripe mangoes, seeded, peeled and chopped
- 150 g chopped red onion
- 85 g diced red pepper
- 75 g golden raisins
- 25 g minced fresh ginger
- ½ teaspoon ground cinnamon
- ¼ teaspoon ground cardamom
- ½ to 1 teaspoon chilli flakes
- 120 ml apple cider vinegar
- 120 ml cup pineapple juice or apple juice
- 100 g sugar
- ½ teaspoon kosher salt

PREP
Place all of the ingredients in the Instant Pot® and stir to combine. Secure the lid on the pot. Close the pressure-release valve.

COOK
Select **MANUAL** and cook at high pressure for 5 minutes. When cooking is complete, use a natural release to depressurise. Press **CANCEL**.

Select **SAUTÉ** and adjust to **LESS**. Cook chutney for 10 minutes or until desired consistency. Press **CANCEL**.

SERVE
Serve with turkey, chicken, pork and ham. Store in a tightly sealed container in the fridge for up to 1 week.

Basics

Pressure-Cooked Chicken Stock

The amount of flavour this stock takes on being cooked under pressure is amazing – without hours of simmering on the hob.

PREP TIME	FUNCTION		CLOSED POT TIME	TOTAL TIME	RELEASE
10 minutes	Soup/Stock		1 hour 40 minutes	1 hour 50 minutes	Natural

MAKES: about 2.25 litres

- 1.1 kg bony chicken pieces (wings, backs and/or necks)
- 3 stalks celery with leaves, cut up
- 2 medium carrots, scrubbed, trimmed and cut in half (leave peel on)
- 1 large onion, unpeeled and cut into large chunks
- 1 medium tomato, halved
- 4 sprigs fresh flat-leaf parsley
- 2 bay leaves
- 4 cloves garlic, unpeeled and lightly crushed
- 1 teaspoon salt
- 1 teaspoon dried sage, thyme or basil, crushed
- ½ teaspoon whole black peppercorns
- 1.8 litres cold water

PREP
If using wings, cut each wing at joints into three pieces. Place chicken pieces in the Instant Pot®. Add celery, carrots, onion, tomato, parsley, bay leaves, garlic, salt, dried herbs, peppercorns and the water. Secure the lid on the pot. Close the pressure-release valve.

COOK
Select **SOUP/STOCK**. When cooking is complete, use a natural release to depressurise.

Remove chicken pieces from pot.* Using a slotted spoon, remove as many vegetables as you can. Line a colander with four layers of muslin. Set colander over a large bowl or casserole and strain stock through muslin; discard vegetables and seasonings.

SERVE
If using the stock immediately, skim the fat from the top. Or chill stock for at least 6 hours. Remove fat with a spoon and discard. Store stock in airtight containers in the fridge for up to 3 days or freeze for 6 months.

*TIP: If desired, remove meat from bones when they are cool enough to handle. Chop the meat and discard the bones. Store meat in an airtight container in the fridge for up to 3 days or freeze for up to 3 months.

Slow-Cooked Chicken Stock

Toss all of the ingredients in the pot in the morning and then walk away. At the end of the day you'll be rewarded with a rich, delicious stock that can be used in soups, stews, risotto and all kinds of other recipes.

PREP TIME	FUNCTION	CLOSED POT TIME	TOTAL TIME
10 minutes	Slow Cook (More)	6 hours	6 hours 10 minutes

MAKES: about 2.25 litres

- 1.1 kg bony chicken pieces (wings, backs and/or necks)
- 3 stalks celery with leaves, cut up
- 2 medium carrots, scrubbed, trimmed and cut in half (leave peel on)
- 1 large onion, unpeeled and cut into large chunks
- 1 medium tomato, halved
- 4 sprigs fresh flat-leaf parsley
- 2 bay leaves
- 4 cloves garlic, unpeeled and lightly crushed
- 1 teaspoon salt
- 1 teaspoon dried sage, thyme or basil, crushed
- ½ teaspoon whole black peppercorns
- 1.9 litres cold water

PREP

If using wings, cut each wing at joints into three pieces. Place chicken pieces in the Instant Pot®. Add celery, carrots, onion, tomato, parsley, bay leaves, garlic, salt, dried herbs, peppercorns and the water. Secure the lid on the pot. Open the pressure-release valve.

COOK

Select **SLOW COOK** and adjust to **MORE**. Cook for 6 hours.

Remove chicken pieces from pot.* Using a slotted spoon, remove as many vegetables as you can. Line a colander with four layers of muslin (or use a fine-mesh strainer). Set colander over a large bowl or casserole and strain stock through muslin; discard vegetables and seasonings.

SERVE

If using the stock immediately, skim the fat from the top. Or chill stock for at least 6 hours. Remove fat with a spoon and discard. Store stock in airtight containers in the fridge for up to 3 days or freeze for 6 months.

*TIP: If desired, remove meat from bones when they are cool enough to handle. Chop the meat and discard the bones. Store meat in an airtight container in the fridge for up to 3 days or freeze for up to 3 months.

Pressure-Cooked Beef Stock

Beef stock can be difficult to make at home and get a good, rich taste. Some recipes call for roasting the bones before making stock to intensify the beefy flavour, but with this recipe, there's no need for that additional step.

PREP TIME	FUNCTION	CLOSED POT TIME	TOTAL TIME	RELEASE
10 minutes	Soup/Stock	3 hours 20 minutes	3 hours 30 minutes	Natural

MAKES: about 2.25 litres

675 g beef soup bones (knuckle, neck and marrow bones)

2 medium carrots, scrubbed, trimmed and cut in half (leave peel on)

1 large onion, unpeeled and cut into large chunks

1 medium leek, white part only, cut into 5-cm chunks

3 stalks celery with leaves, cut up

1 tablespoon dried thyme, crushed

1½ teaspoons salt

1 teaspoon whole black peppercorns

8 sprigs fresh flat-leaf parsley

2 bay leaves

4 cloves garlic, unpeeled and lightly crushed

2 litres cold water

1 tablespoon cider vinegar

PREP
Combine bones, carrots, onion, leek, celery, thyme, salt, peppercorns, parsley, bay leaves, garlic, the water and the vinegar in the Instant Pot®.

COOK
Secure the lid on the pot. Close the pressure-release valve. Select **SOUP/STOCK** and adjust cook time to 120 minutes. When cooking is complete, use a natural release to depressurise.

Remove bones from stock.* Using a slotted spoon, remove as many vegetables as you can. Line a colander with four layers of muslin. Set colander over a large bowl or casserole and strain stock through muslin; discard vegetables and seasonings.

SERVE
If using the stock immediately, skim the fat from the top. Or chill stock for at least 6 hours. Remove fat with a spoon and discard. Store stock in an airtight container in the fridge for up to 3 days or freeze for 6 months.

*TIP: If desired, remove meat from bones when they are cool enough to handle. Chop the meat and discard the bones. Store meat in airtight containers in the fridge for up to 3 days or freeze for up to 3 months.

Slow-Cooked Beef Stock

A little bit of vinegar helps draw minerals out of the bones as they simmer in the liquid, making the finished stock more flavourful and nutrient-rich.

PREP TIME	FUNCTION	CLOSED POT TIME	TOTAL TIME
10 minutes	Slow Cook (More)	8 hours	8 hours 10 minutes

MAKES: about 1.5 litres

- 675 g beef soup bones (knuckle, neck and marrow bones)
- 2 medium carrots, scrubbed and trimmed (leave peel on)
- 1 large onion, unpeeled and cut into large chunks
- 1 medium leek, white part only, cut into 5-cm chunks
- 3 stalks celery with leaves, cut up
- 1 tablespoon dried thyme, crushed
- 1½ teaspoons salt
- 1 teaspoon whole black peppercorns
- 8 sprigs fresh flat-leaf parsley
- 2 bay leaves
- 4 cloves garlic, unpeeled and lightly crushed
- 2 litres cold water
- 1 tablespoon cider vinegar

PREP
Combine bones, carrots, onion, leek, celery, thyme, salt, peppercorns, parsley, bay leaves, garlic, the water and the vinegar in the Instant Pot®.

COOK
Secure the lid on the pot. Open the pressure-release valve. Select **SLOW COOK** and adjust to **MORE**. Cook for 8 hours.

Remove bones from stock.* Using a slotted spoon, remove as many vegetables as you can. Line a colander with four layers of muslin. Set colander over a large bowl or casserole and strain stock through muslin; discard vegetables and seasonings.

SERVE
If using the stock immediately, skim the fat from the top. Or chill stock for at least 6 hours. Remove fat with a spoon and discard. Store stock in airtight containers in the fridge for up to 3 days or freeze for 6 months.

*TIP: If desired, remove meat from bones when they are cool enough to handle. Chop the meat and discard the bones. Store meat in airtight containers in the fridge for up to 3 days or freeze for up to 3 months.

Dark Vegetable Stock

This richly flavoured vegan stock is infused with the earthy essence of mushrooms. Use it in soups or stews–or sip on a cup of it alone as an energising hot beverage.

PREP TIME	FUNCTION	CLOSED POT TIME	TOTAL TIME	RELEASE
20 minutes	Sauté (Normal); Pressure/Manual (High)	60 minutes	1 hour 20 minutes	Natural

MAKES: about 1.9 litres

- 1 tablespoon olive oil
- 2 red onions, peeled and quartered
- 3 cloves garlic, smashed
- 2 carrots, peeled and coarsely chopped
- 50 g shiitake mushroom stems (from about 16 mushrooms) or 4 whole dried shiitake mushrooms
- 175 g cremini or shiitake mushrooms, sliced
- 2 celery stalks with leaves, chopped
- 1 sprig rosemary
- 3 sprigs thyme
- 2 bay leaves
- ¼ teaspoon whole black peppercorns
- 1.9 litres water
- ½ teaspoon salt

PREP

Select **SAUTÉ** on the Instant Pot® and adjust to **NORMAL**. When hot, add the oil. Add the onions and cook for 4 minutes.* Add the garlic and cook 6 minutes longer or until the onions start turning brown. Press **CANCEL**. Add carrots, shiitake mushrooms, cremini mushrooms, celery, rosemary, thyme, bay leaves, peppercorns and the water. Secure the lid on the pot. Close the pressure-release valve.

COOK

Select **MANUAL** and cook at high pressure for 10 minutes. When cooking is complete, use a natural release to depressurise.

SERVE

Pour stock through a strainer, pressing on the solids with a spoon to extract all the liquid and flavour. Stir salt into the stock.

Use immediately or store in a tightly covered container in the fridge for up to 1 week or for up to 3 months in the freezer.

***NOTE:** The onion and hot oil will spatter a bit while it's being sautéed.

Jill Nussinow blogs at TheVeggieQueen.com and is the author of *Vegan Under Pressure*.

Perfectly Cooked Eggs

Steaming eggs in the shell gives you the very best results, whether you want soft-, medium-, or hard-cooked eggs. An extra benefit of steaming: your hard-cooked eggs will never acquire a green ring around the yolk—a sign of overcooking.

PREP TIME	FUNCTION	CLOSED POT TIME	TOTAL TIME	RELEASE
5 minutes	Manual/Pressure (Low)	Varies	Varies	Natural

SERVES: Varies

240 ml water

1 to 6 large eggs

PREP
Pour the water into the Instant Pot®. Place a steamer basket or the trivet in the pot. Carefully arrange eggs in the steamer basket. Secure the lid on the pot. Close the pressure-release valve.

COOK
For soft-cooked eggs, select **MANUAL** and cook at low pressure for 3 minutes. When cooking time is complete, use a natural release to depressurise. (For medium-cooked eggs, cook for 4 minutes; for hard-cooked eggs, cook for 5 minutes.)

SERVE
Remove the lid from the pot and gently place eggs in a bowl of cool water for 1 minute to serve warm.

Classic Porridge

Get this porridge cooking before you jump in the shower. By the time you're ready for the day, your porridge will be ready for you.

PREP TIME	FUNCTION	CLOSED POT TIME	TOTAL TIME	RELEASE
5 minutes	Manual/Pressure (High	10 minutes	15 minutes	Natural

SERVES: 2 or 3

Non-stick cooking spray

480 ml water

480 ml unsweetened plain or vanilla almond, soy or cashew milk (or 240 ml non-dairy milk and 240 ml water)

⅛ teaspoon salt

100 g rolled oats

1 tablespoon butter (optional)

½ teaspoon vanilla extract (optional)

¼ teaspoon ground cinnamon (optional)

1 tablespoon honey, pure maple syrup or agave nectar (optional)

35 g raisins, dried cranberries, dried cherries or chopped dried apricots (optional)

3 tablespoons chopped toasted almonds, walnuts or pecans (optional)

PREP

Spray the inner pot of the Instant Pot® with cooking spray (this helps reduce foaming and aids in cleanup). Pour the 480 ml water into the Instant Pot®. Place the trivet in the pot. Place a 1.9-litre heatproof bowl on top of the trivet. Combine the water, milk, salt and oats in the bowl. Secure the lid on the pot. Close the pressure-release valve.

COOK

Select **MANUAL** and cook at high pressure for 5 minutes. When cooking is complete, use a natural release to depressurise.

SERVE

If desired, stir in the butter, vanilla, cinnamon, sweetener, dried fruit and nuts. Top with additional milk (dairy or non-dairy) if desired.

Oatmeal

It's important to use a non-dairy milk in this oatmeal because the natural sugars in cow's milk will cause it to scorch. Top the cooked oatmeal with dairy milk if you like.

PREP TIME	FUNCTION	CLOSED POT TIME	TOTAL TIME	RELEASE
5 minutes	Manual/Pressure (High)	20 minutes	25 minutes	Natural

SERVES: 4 to 6

Non-stick cooking spray

480 ml water

240 ml unsweetened plain or vanilla almond, soy, or cashew milk

⅛ teaspoon salt

160 g porridge oats

2 tablespoons butter (optional)

1 teaspoon vanilla extract (optional)

1 teaspoon ground cinnamon (optional)

1 tablespoon to 2 tablespoons honey, brown sugar, pure maple syrup or agave nectar (optional)

50 g raisins, dried cranberries, dried cherries or chopped dried apricots (optional)

30 g chopped toasted almonds, walnuts or pecans (optional)

Milk (optional)

PREP

Spray the inner pot of the Instant Pot® with cooking spray (this helps reduce foaming and aids in cleanup). Combine the water, milk, salt and oats in the pot. Secure the lid on the pot. Close the pressure-release valve.

COOK

Select **MANUAL** and cook at high pressure for 10 minutes. When cooking is complete, use a natural release to depressurise. (If oats are not tender, place the lid on the pot and let stand for 5 to 10 minutes.)

SERVE

If desired, stir in the butter, vanilla, cinnamon, sweetener, dried fruit and nuts. Top with additional milk if desired.

Homemade Yogurt

When you open the pot after 8 hours of incubation, the yogurt will appear very firm and the whey–a pale yellow liquid–will be separate from the milk solids. Just give the mixture a stir before you pour into the strainer.

PREP TIME	FUNCTION	CLOSED POT TIME	TOTAL TIME	RELEASE
5 minutes	Steam; Yogurt	9 hours	9 hours 5 minutes + 6 hours chill	Quick

MAKES: about 2.25 litres

710 ml water

4.5 litres milk (whole, semi-skimmed or skimmed)*

3 tablespoons powdered milk (optional)

55 g plain, unsweetened yogurt with active cultures

Vanilla (1 or 2 tablespoons extract or 1 vanilla bean, split and scraped) (optional)

100 g granulated sugar or honey (optional)

Muslin

PREP
To sterilise the Instant Pot®, pour the water into the pot. Secure the lid on the pot. Close the pressure-release valve. Select **STEAM** and adjust cooking time to 5 minutes. When cooking time is complete, use a quick-release to depressurise. Press **CANCEL**. Remove the lid and pour water out of the pot. Dry and cool pot.

COOK
Pour the milk into the completely cooled pot. Stir in powdered milk if using. Secure the lid on the pot. Open the pressure-release valve. Select **YOGURT** and adjust until display reads 'Boil'.

When boil and cool-down cycles are complete (about 1 hour), check the temperature with an instant-read thermometer. If it is not 85°C/185°F, select **SAUTÉ** and adjust to **NORMAL** to warm it to 85°C/185°F. Press **CANCEL**. Remove inner pot and place on a cooling rack to cool. (Or speed the cooling process by setting the inner pot into a sink full of cool water.) Cool milk to 45°C/110°F, whisking occasionally. Return inner pot to Instant Pot®.

Whisk in yogurt and, if desired, vanilla and sugar. Secure the lid on the pot. Open the pressure-release valve. Select **YOGURT** and adjust incubation time to 8 hours, making sure display says **NORMAL**. (If a more tart flavour is desired, you can adjust the time up to 10 hours.)

When incubation time is complete, cool yogurt in the pot in the fridge, covered and undisturbed, for at least 6 hours or overnight.

In a large bowl place a colander lined with a double layer of muslin. Transfer yogurt to the muslin-lined strainer and strain in the fridge for about 1 to 2 hours for ordinary yogurt or at least 8 hours or overnight for Greek-style yogurt. Store in tightly sealed containers in the fridge.

SERVE
Enjoy yogurt plain or with fruit, preserves, nuts or granola.

*NOTE: Milk that is higher in fat will produce thicker, creamier yogurt than semi-skimmed or skimmed milk–but you can also thicken yogurt by straining it for a longer period of time. The powdered milk is optional, but it, too, helps thicken the yogurt–as well as adding protein.

Pressure-Cooking Charts

Because people have preferences in the taste and texture of their foods, these timings offer a range so you can experiment and find the timings you like. All are based on the high-pressure setting.

Fish & Shellfish

Cook times are generally short to preserve the delicate flavours and textures. Steaming is the ideal method, though it does depend somewhat on the recipe. You will need at least 240 ml of water in the bottom of the pot and the trivet and/or a vegetable steamer basket. Use a quick release.

Fish & Shellfish	Fresh Cooking Time (minutes)	Frozen Cooking Time (minutes)
Crab	3–4	5–6
Fish, whole	5–6	7–10
Fish, fillet	2–3	3–4
Fish, steak	3–4	4–6
Lobster	3–4	4–6
Mussels	2–3	4–5
Seafood soup or stock	6–7	7–9
Prawns	1–2	2–3

Poultry

In general, removing the skin from poultry before pressure cooking yields the best results. Raw poultry is highly perishable. Never set the delay cook time for more than 1 hour. We recommend instead cooking the poultry immediately and using the **KEEP WARM** function to maintain food at serving temperature. Use a natural release for larger, bone-in pieces and a quick release for smaller, boneless pieces.

Poultry	Cooking Time (minutes)
Chicken, breasts	8–10
Chicken, whole	20–25
Chicken, dark meat	10–15
Duck, cut up with bones	10–12
Duck, whole	25–30
Pheasant	20–25
Poussin, whole	10–15

Poultry	Cooking Time (minutes)
Turkey, boneless breast	15–20
Turkey breast, whole with bones	25–30
Turkey, drumsticks	15–20
Quail, whole	8–10

Rice & Grains

The pre-set **RICE** and **MULTIGRAIN** functions generally provide the optimum timing for cooking rice and other grains, but the **MANUAL** setting may also be used. Use **the following grain:** water ratios. Use a natural release.

Rice & Grains	Grain to Water Ratio (cups)	Cooking Time (minutes)
Type		
Barley, pearl	1:4	25–30
Barley, pot	1:3–1:4	25–30
Couscous	1:2	5–8
Kamut, whole	1:3	10–12
Millet	1: 1⅔	10–12
Oats, quick-cooking	1: 1⅔	6
Oats, porridge	1: 1⅔	10
Quinoa	1:2	8
Rice, basmati	1: 1½	4–8
Rice, brown	1: 1¼	22–28
Rice, jasmine	1:1	4–10
Rice, white	1: 1½	8
Rice, wild	1:3	25–30
Sorghum	1:3	20–25
Spelt berries	1:3	15–20
Wheat berries	1:3	25–30

Vegetables

Steaming vegetables–whether fresh or frozen–helps preserve vitamin and minerals, as well as maintain their bright colours and crisp-tender textures. When steaming vegetables, you need at least 240 ml of water in the bottom of the pot and the trivet and/or a vegetable steamer basket. Use a quick release.

Vegetables	Fresh Cooking Time (minutes)	Frozen Cooking Time (minutes)
Artichoke, whole, trimmed	9–11	11–13
Artichoke, hearts	4–5	5–6
Asparagus, whole or cut	1–2	2–3
Aubergines, slices or chunks	2–3	4–5
Beans, green/yellow, whole, ends trimmed	1–2	2–3
Beetroots, small, whole	11–13	13–15
Beetroots, large, whole	20–25	25–30
Broccoli, florets	2–3	3–4
Broccoli, stalks	3–4	4–5
Brussels sprouts, whole	3–4	4–5
Cabbage, red or green, shredded	2–3	3–4
Cabbage, red or green, wedges	3–4	4–5
Carrots, sliced or shredded	1–2	2–3
Carrots, whole or chunks	2–3	3–4
Cauliflower florets	2–3	3–4
Celery, chunks	2–3	3–4
Corn, kernels	1–2	2–3
Corn, on the cob	3–4	4–5
Endive	1–2	2–3
Escarole, chopped	1–2	2–3
Greens (beetroots, spring greens, kale, spinach, Swiss chard, turnip greens), chopped	3–6	4–7

Vegetables	Fresh Cooking Time (minutes)	Frozen Cooking Time (minutes)
Leeks	2–4	3–5
Mixed vegetables	2–3	3–4
Okra	2–3	3–4
Onions, sliced	2–3	3–4
Parsnips, sliced	2–3	2–3
Parsnips, chunks	2–4	4–6
Peas, mangetout or sugar snap	1–2	2–3
Peas, green	1–2	2–3
Potatoes, cubed	7–9	9–11
Potatoes, whole, baby	10–12	12–14
Potatoes, whole, large	12–15	15–19
Pumpkin, small slices or chunks	4–5	6–7
Pumpkin, large slices or chunks	8–10	10–14
Spinach	1–2	3–4
Spring greens	4–5	5–6
Squash, acorn, slices or chunks	6–7	8–9
Squash, butternut, slices or chunks	8–10	10–12
Swede, slices	3–5	4–6
Swede, chunks	4–6	6–8
Sweet potato, cubed	7–9	9–11
Sweet potato, whole, small	10–12	12–14
Sweet potato, whole, large	12–15	15–19
Sweet pepper, slices or chunks	1–3	2–4
Tomatoes, quartered	2–3	4–5

Meat

Browning meats on the **SAUTÉ** setting before pressure cooking helps to seal in the juices. Raw meat is highly perishable. Never set the delay cook time for more than 1 to 2 hours. We recommend instead cooking the meat immediately and using the **KEEP WARM** function to maintain food at serving temperature. Use a natural release for larger cuts and a quick release for smaller cuts.

Meat	Cooking Time (minutes)
Type	
Beef, stewing steak	15–20
Beef, meatballs	10–15
Beef, whole: pot roast, steak, rump, round, chuck, blade or brisket	35–40
Beef, small chunks: pot roast, steak, rump, chuck, blade or brisket	25–30
Beef, ribs	25–30
Beef, shanks	25–30
Beef, oxtail	40–50
Ham, slice	9–12
Ham, shoulder	25–30
Pork, loin	45–50
Pork, shoulder	55–60
Pork, ribs	20–25
Lamb, stewing steak	10–15
Lamb, leg	35–45
Veal, chop	5–8
Veal, roast	35–45

Fruit

Steaming fresh or dried fruits best preserves their taste, texture and nutrients. When steaming fruits, you need at least 240 ml of water in the bottom of the pot and the trivet and/or a vegetable steamer basket. Use a quick release.

Fruits	Fresh Cooking Time (minutes)	Dried Cooking Time (minutes)
Apples, slices or pieces	2–3	3–4
Apples, whole	3–4	4–6
Apricots, whole or halves	2–3	3–4
Peaches	2–3	4–6
Pears, whole	3–4	4–6
Pears, slices or halves	2–3	4–5
Plums	2–3	4–5 (prunes)
Raisins	N/A	4–5

Dried Beans, Peas & Lentils

Dried beans double in volume and weight after soaking or cooking. Do not fill the inner pot more than half full to allow for expansion. Use enough liquid to cover the beans. Use a natural release.

Dried Beans, Peas & Lentils	Dry Cooking Time (minutes)	Soaked Cooking Times (minutes)
Type		
Adzuki beans	20–25	10–15
Black beans	20–25	10–15
Black-eyed peas	20–25	10–15
Broad beans	20–25	10–15
Chickpeas	35–40	20–25
Cannellini beans	35–40	20–25
Pigeon peas	20–25	15–20
Lentils, Puy	15–20	N/A
Lentils, green/brown	15–20	N/A
Lentils, yellow, split (moong dal)	15–18	N/A
Kidney beans, red	25–30	20–25
Kidney beans, white	35–40	20–25
Pinto beans	25–30	20–25
Scarlet runner beans	20–25	10–15
Soy beans	25–30	20–25

Index

(italic page numbers refer to photographs)